WALKING BACKWARDS
or,
The Magical Art of Psychedelic Psychogeography

Copyright 2018 Part I Julian Vayne
Copyright 2018 Part II Greg Humphries

Second Edition 2018
Published by The Universe Machine, Norwich

ISBN 978-0-9954904-8-2

Designed by Francesca Stella

Cover Illustration:
The World Turn'd Upside Down, Cornwall, 2017
Greg Humphries
Private Collection

Book Illustrations:
Greg Humphries

Prayer of Thanksgiving
To my great friend and companion Greg Humphries; I rejoice that we have walked so far and so long together.
I give thanks to those spirits in many forms who teach me, and to the Great Mystery for arising into the awesome reality of this world.
I give thanks for the opportunity to share my journey with others and for the care and love of my community that makes this possible.
Ahoy!
Julian Vayne

Prayer of Thanksgiving
To Joolz and all the journeys of Mystery and Art we travel together,
To Fran for walking the path of love with me,
To Nikki for her eagle eyed compassionate weaving of words,
To Eleanor for the chance to open my heart,
And the Bump for the excitement and trepidation of what's over the next horizon.
Greg Humphries

CONTENTS

Part I - Julian Vayne — 1

Of Thought and Memory — 2
- The Way Of The Wanderer — 4
- Shrine Making — 5
- Offerings — 5
- Artworks — 5
- Right Way of Walking — 6
- Entheogens — 7
- Song and Sound — 8
- Hiding Things — 9
- Eating and Drinking — 9

Backsighting — 12
The Psychedelic Landscape — 14
The Art of Walking — 16

Part II - Greg Humphries — 19

Prologue — 21
The Walks — 31
- HARTLAND POINT — 33
- *Albion Awake!* — 41
- ROUGHTOR — 57
- *Song For The Dead* — 58

Part III - Photographs — 91

- HARTLAND POINT — 92
- ROUGHTOR — 110

PART I
Julian Vayne
Devon 2016

Of Thought And Memory

Recalling how memory works; long buried stories and fragmentary images are brought back into awareness, summoned from the unconscious, perhaps by a landscape, other times by a chance phrase, or even the taste of a biscuit. Memories, of my psychogeographical explorations, are awoken by the chance discovery by Greg of the photographs in this book.

Photographs themselves are magical things; patterns of light frozen at a certain moment, fixed into solid and enduring form. These pictures of the past easily light the touch paper of memory. The images here seem to me to be both fresh and vivid, and simultaneously improbably old. For starters these photographs were taken on real film, and indeed some were shot on a Polaroid style camera. This technology allowed Greg and me, as part of our walk on Bodmin Moor, to leave a pictorial trail for others to follow. In homage to Kit William's Masquerade, we left a hidden prize for subsequent travellers to find, providing a clue at another location by leaving a Polaroid of me pointing towards the granite tor where we had secreted the treasure.

But beyond the evocation of personal memory, these images allow me to reflect on the practice of psychogeography itself. These photographs record two walks, two chapters in a much longer oeuvre, a walk through the magic of our landscape that is still ongoing.

The British, or more specifically the English countryside, has always been an important source of inspiration for Greg and me.

For both of us there is that sense that the landscape we encounter is deeply magical. Though there may be the potential perception of our island as a humdrum, overly-familiar place, peek beneath this surface and there is a wonderland right here, right now. Like those mysterious, liminal worlds presented in the novels of Alan Garner, the magical happens both within, and gives rise to the outer world we are familiar with.

'Magical' is one of the words we use to describe our reaction to this refreshed perception. Switching our attention from the preoccupied, reduced awareness that can become a deadly habit, we discover that which is amazing, fabulous, and miraculous even, rooted in the firm reality of our environment. Through the magic of psychogeographical adventures, trees cease to be mute wood, and are transformed into wise Entish guardians. Birds describe omens in their flight patterns; the landscape is the body of a recumbent Goddess. We use skilful means to re-enchant our place and reveal the wonder of our world. In this way we return to a child-like simplicity where, like Taoist masters or unschooled children, we recognize the magic of existence. This is re-enchantment of the world that serves to supplant bland explanationism and eliminate jaded perception.

Magic is also an 'occult practice', something I like to imagine as that body of techniques, found in many cultural settings (religion, psychology, heresy, parapsychology and more) with which we can explore our agency as makers of meaning within the universe we inhabit. In many cultural paradigms (often those of 'spirituality' or 'religion') we can, more or less overtly, find practical 'how to' instructions on how to make this assay into the Mystery.

Methods such as dancing, pain, drumming, prayer, isolation, sex, ceremonial drama and psychedelic drugs are just a few tactics for pursuing this exploration. These methods, while they may be embedded in systems of thought with various theological notions about the relationship between matter and spirit, are embodied practices. Whether we consider yin-style, catabolic approaches— silent meditation, retreat and celibacy—or the yang-style anabolic methods—dancing, communal ritual and orgiastic sex—all these paths lead awareness from the personal field of volitional experience (our bodyminds) towards the Mystery.

The Way of the Wanderer

Walking through a landscape is of course a means of embodied exploration of physical and intrasubjective territories. By walking, with a magical intention or attitude, we actively invoke the mythic reality of what we experience as we stroll in the Mystery of existence. Signs, objects, relationships, time, all these things slip into a synesthetic morphing matrix of the poetic truth of the journey. Everything is charged with hyper-real meaning, but this meaning isn't necessarily fixed. Instead it may flip-flop, dissolve and recombine, go in a second from deeply significant to utterly ridiculous. There may be, of course, no single or ultimate truth. (As magicians, informed by postmodern, pragmatically punk, delightfully Discordian Chaos Magic, Greg and I are not strangers to the idea that the divine and the daft may be one and the same.)

During any psychogeographical journey Greg and I employ a variety of methods to change our awareness, to invoke this magic. I've written about some of the approaches we use previously in *Wanton Green: Contemporary Pagan Writings On Place*.

Shrine Making

Found objects, and others brought along expressly for the purpose, can be used to honour the local spirits. Shrines are built, little altars dressed with flowers, coloured wool, trinkets, and offerings of money and joints. Such interventions serve to mark our sacred attention to the landscape and leave a trail of ritual that, I hope, enhances the journey of those who subsequently discover them. Tiny transient mementos of meditations which punctuate the ritual walk.

On fences, ribbons may be tied, grasses woven with spells through the mesh, and feathers stuck in the gaps between brickwork. Our magick seeks out these crevices in the works of man, as unstoppable and temporary as a mushroom that pushes out of the gap between paving slabs.

Offerings

A shrine is a species of offering. A marking not of territory but of sacredness. Offerings can also be made to gatekeepers and sacred spots. Candles are left at wells along with silver coins (and wishes). Blood may need to be spilt, or tobaccos placed under the earth.

Artworks

Inspired by Andy Goldsworthy, leaves can be laid in a line. Graduations of colour, from green to autumn reds mark this out as the work of man. The large rounded grey pebbles of the North Devon coast can be arranged so that the veins of quartz crystals within them line up. These bright white lines snake across the beach, creating an order which is distinctly human. Or they may be piled up, balanced on top of each other (I once saw a beach on the Isle of Agnes in the Scillies that had hundreds of such piles, a sculptured landscape).

Drawing and painting on surfaces—abandoned signs, great rocks—can also be a way of honouring the spirit of place. (Although I usually content myself with chalk rather than spray paint.)

Right Way of Walking

The terrain offers many ways of locomotion. Walking up a hill, head down looking just a few feet ahead, against the solid wind. Then, looking down from a high place once a vantage point is attained. In this way we go from the view of the mouse to that of the hawk. Once Greg and I climbed a slope covered in heathers and moss. Pawing over the luxurious hair on the pubic mound of a huge goddess. Sniffing her, feeling her wiry fur. So absorbed were we in this erotic close contact that it was only when the ground ran out that we realised we'd crawled to the top of a huge sea cliff. Over the sharp edge was the glittering ocean and air.

Then there is the part of the walk that is real Work. The interminable slog back to the car along the unrelenting metalled road. The final push to get to the peak before we can rest and take it all in. Walking can be a challenging business.

Entheogens

Taken indoors, entheogens tend towards introspection or group consciousness if used as part of a communal ceremony. Outside they allow us to see the fantastic beauty of nature through fresh eyes. We slow down; take everything in. Tufts of dune grass blowing in the sun become the tousled hair of bleached blond surfers. Rivers are appreciated as the veins of the planet. Birds become messengers from other worlds. We see in a way that is both hyper-symbolized and yet somehow also shorn of preconceptions. We focus on those aspects of the land that have something to teach us. I spent one journey obsessed by 'the edge', the razor cut sheering away of cliffs. The point at which the sea and the land and sky all meet. Entheogens adjust our perception so that we are seeing the liminal, the within and the without as they meet.

Of course one must judge the dose well, especially if interaction with other people or negotiating dangerous landscapes is required. LSD, mushrooms and other tryptamines are wonderful spirits to go walking with. As one commentator put it;

"But they (drugs) all do sort of the same thing, and that is rearrange what you thought was real, and they remind you of the beauty of pretty simple things. You forget, because you're so busy going from A to Z, that there's 24 letters in between..."

The term 'museum level' has been used to describe the dose of a psychoactive where one might be able to function successfully in a social space (for example a visit to a gallery or cream-tea shop) and not be so wired that you get thrown out (or become reduced to a paranoid wreck). Museum level is ideal for walking. One may also use those shorter acting substances (for example smoked DMTs) at the peak of a journey. Clearly one should find a safe environment within which to take these substances since they can be temporarily incapacitating. Proximity to cliffs and mine shafts is to be avoided!

Song and Sound

Another archaic technique of ecstasy. Whether it be listening hard to the sound of your own feet on the earth, humming or singing as one walks, or perhaps using mantra and vibrated words of power at stops along the route. Making sounds, we contribute to the soundscape of a place. By inducing trance, rhythmic sound can help us to focus deeply on one aspect of a location (playing with echoes and percussive sounds is an excellent way to do this). As we become ecstatic, literally standing outside of ourselves, our perspective can shift. We are no longer beings walking on the land; instead we are in it and of it.

Prayer and words of power can be spoken at sacred locations; lone trees, crossroads, bridges. We can program ourselves with spelling, sounding out our intentions as we send driftwood wands out to sea, or touch sacred objects; megaliths, doorways, windmills.

It's good to save words at some points in a magical walk. Make times when chit chat is minimized. Walk in silence and only talk when you are moved to do so by deep unconscious forces. Make sounds in reply to the wind and talk to the animals and plants with respectful, measured dialogue. This way the act of speaking is potentiated.

Listening is also enhanced this way. And if there is conversation it should be remembered that this is a special space and words should be chosen with flare and care.

Hiding Things

Talismans, witch bottles, runes and tokens can be buried and secreted along the journey. These act as gnostic strange attractors, linking your power to the place you have visited.

Eating and Drinking

It's possible, even on an urban walk in all but the most densely populated areas, to find wild foods to eat. Seaweeds, blackberries, the cucumbery taste of fleshy navelwort, the coconut dryness of gorse flowers. Eating the landscape it literally becomes you. Drinking from a stream where the water is fresh, tasting the brine of the sea. Getting all gustatory with the planet is good for the mind, body and soul. It also leaves you with a nice feeling that if the total breakdown of civilisation happens anytime soon you'll be able to survive for awhile at least.

These days Greg and I are able to share some of these techniques with others in our professional work. While some practices (like the use of mind-bending drugs) are prohibited by the caring laws of the State, others are more readily accessible. Greg's work as artist and art educator and mine as writer and cultural learning consultant, allow us to introduce other people to the methods we employ to break the mindset of the familiar and to re-experience the magic of reality.

These are methods to change our Set and Setting, to stimulate curiosity and encourage us to engage with our immediate environment.

Since the tradition of chaos magic which Greg and myself share places an emphasis on 'how to' information, here are a few (non-entheogenic) examples of techniques you might like to try on your own psychogeographic journeys.

Stop—listen for five natural sounds. What can you hear? Which sounds do you consider 'natural'?

As you walk become aware that your feet are pointing down towards the molten core of our planet and your head is pointing out towards the vast blackness of interstellar space. Be aware of the reality of this situation, now.

Take a deep breath and as you breathe out turn around, try to keep breathing out as you circle 360 degrees; what can you see around your horizon?

As you breathe out, be aware that the plants around you are taking in your carbon dioxide. Notice how the plants are made from solidified atmospheric carbon, they are crystallized air. Go and breathe directly on a plant and make that connection an explicit, embodied truth.

Look for animal and vehicle tracks, animal spoor and trails through the grass, who has passed this way before you? A cyclist, deer, perhaps even a tiger?

Use your hands as you walk touch what you pass, walls, trees, grasses, the earth etc., pay attention to your feet also. Verbally name each texture or sensation for a period of your journey; soft, unyielding, smooth, warm etc.

Backsighting

Many of the photographs in this volume are examples of backsighting views. These images record what we have done before, the art we have made at important points on our journey. Like the speakers of Aymara, an Indian language of the high Andes, our past is in front of us (rather than metaphorically behind us) as both art and photographic record.

Backsighting is the navigational practice of periodically looking over your shoulder as you travel a route. This simple trick helps if you need to retrace your steps; you know what to look for when you're going the opposite way.

When we look back, when we remember a route, most of us recall what we call landmarks. These are sometimes the infection of written signage that proliferates in the British landscape. On my island we have lettered signs everywhere, from the municipal postwar sigils of the Highway Code, all the way back to letters risted on Iron Age marker stones. Yet wordy signs, 'N miles to Whatever', handy though they are, are generally less easily recalled than things — the ruined church, the crossroads, the bridge over the river, the huge yew tree, the swelling round barrows on the horizon hills.

When we consider those other landmarks what might be our key images? Could we create a psychogeographical tarot? What would be the arcanum of the dérive, or a Qabalah of walking?

The Walker
The Doorway

The Path
The Crossroads
The Water
The Tree
The Bridge
The Resting Place
The High Place
[...]

We could perhaps develop this symbolic vocabulary of liminal spaces and landmarks to include other actors and scenes on our journey:

The Companion
The Encounter
The Difficult Passage
The Light
The Nourishing
The Obstruction
[...]

The ritual of psychogeography includes a keen awareness of these landmarks, characters and events. It is often at these significant locations or moments on a walk when Greg and I deploy one of our awareness-altering approaches mentioned above; we engineer our context by deploying methods of changing awareness in site-specific ways. We reach the crossroads and, not only do we deal with the pragmatic necessity of selecting our road, but we also respond to this place and attempt to make contact in some way with its genius loci. We may create art at these points in the walk, perhaps sing or otherwise use words to witness the importance of that landmark, tuning in, to use a popular vernacular, to the energy of the place.

The Psychedelic Landscape

Those wonderful medicines which we name the psychedelics are the core of the practice that Greg and I share. Whether the agent is one prepared from a plant, or cooked up in an alchemist's laboratory, employing psychedelics is, for us, a favoured method of altering our awareness. While both of us are schooled in various traditions of martial arts, yogic and meditative practices, and several sorts of contemporary, typically non-entheogenic ritual practice (such as Wicca and Druidry); the fact is that these marvellous medicines are very important elements in the magic we do.

Recent brain imaging studies have, perhaps unsurprisingly, confirmed what people have been subjectively reporting ever since that first stoned ape ate a mushroom. Put in simplified neurological terms; psychedelic drugs stimulate systems in the brain that are typically down-regulated in 'normal' waking awareness and simultaneously reduce the activity of those regions that are 'normally' active. Meanwhile, as the graphic equaliser of brain activity harmonizes the activity of the alert and quiescent parts of the brain, the connectivity between regions massively increases. Bits of the brain that normally don't 'talk' to each other find themselves connected and communicating. Old habituated patterns break down to be replaced by novel, weird, amazing, sometimes frightening new connections. The mind changes from a single processor that gives rise to a more-or-less robotic 'self', to a massive parallel processing system capable of delivering a psychedelicized awareness.

This psychedelic awareness has all kinds of possibilities embedded within. In therapeutic contexts the fact that psychedelics disrupt old cognitive patterns and create new connections means that patients can find new ways of understanding their problems. Post-traumatic stress disorder, substance additions or childhoods of abusive parenting; these and other difficulties respond well to psychedelic therapy, as data from both the first wave of psychedelic research, and the more recent studies of the 'psychedelic renaissance', demonstrate.

Magicians are apt to contend that, 'as above, so below, as within so without'. Given these Hermetic axioms, the prospect of using substances that demonstrably facilitate the joining up of previously discrete regions of the mind is an attractive prospect.

In addition to the mental health benefits, psychedelics can help us problem solve and, with the right dosage, set and setting, can give us visions of the divine (which is nice). They may also enhance processes that are best described in (para) psychological language. Spells are cast, telepathy happens, the future is foretold, synchronicitous events slot into place 'just so'.

And not least: The psychedelic experience, especially in the context of landscape is potentially sublime; awe-inspiring, majestic and typically full of heart-breaking beauty. The psychedelic imagination opens a whole aesthetic of the supra-normal consciousness of our environment; what's not to like about that?

The Art Of Walking

I look back at these images. At my leather-coat wearing, sunglass sporting self of some fifteen years ago. Greg is hidden behind the camera as both bone fide man of mystery and also as the photographer capturing most of the images from these walks.

Since those days, when Greg's art was being strongly influenced by his early encounter with ayahuasca, his work has developed in some wonderful ways. While he still draws and makes images like the ones in this volume, he is also to be found fashioning beautiful mythical objects from a (re)imagined Albion. His latest work, after Blake's poem Jerusalem, is a handmade hunting bow, burnished with gold. The twelve arrows of desire are likewise exquisitely handcrafted.

My art is mostly the creation of texts, of writing. As I look back on those walks at Hartland and on Bodmin, I'm reminded of the things I've written since then, including meditations following subsequent psychogeographical journeys.

For instance several years ago I wrote an essay, inspired by my own psychogeography and the work of Ramsey Dukes (The Magickal Data Tsunami published in *Chaos Craft*). In it I discuss how being out in nature provides us with a cognitively rich environment which feels good. While we may think of our time in the woods as 'getting away from it all', in fact this is, in terms of incoming sensory data, quite the reverse. We can see more greens in the trees than are possible on our computer monitors, we hear the fabulously complex sound of the nearby waterfall, our bodies get the interconnected feedback of wind, the uneven earth underfoot, variable humidity and more.

Being 'in nature' (and we can debate exactly what we mean by 'nature' until the wild horses or domesticated cows come home…) is to be enriched. This is especially true if we open our senses (through whatever techniques we prefer) and, like the psychedelicized brain, gain a perspective that is relational and interconnected.

The Magickal Data Tsunami was written after a visit to St. Nectan's Glen in North Cornwall, a site that these days I am closely associated with as psychogeographer, Pagan, and in a professional capacity too. One of the photographs unearthed for this book is of St. Nectan's Well, somewhat further up the coast, near Hartland. It would seem that years later I am still connected to the mythos of this Saxon Saint.

For both Greg and me, expressing our engagement with the landscape through a creative praxis is vitally important. We articulate insights from our walks in text and images, as both a practice in itself and a reflection of our journeys. In time we set off again, into the magical territory, finding the new as well as the deeply familiar, our intention to re-enchant the world for ourselves and to share this with others.

I hope you enjoy what we have shared in this book, that it inspires your psychogeographical explorations, and encourages your own creative reflections on what you discover along the path.

Julian Vayne
Devon 2016

PART II
Greg Humphries
Cornwall 2016

"And did those feet in ancient time,
Walk upon England's mountains green:
And was the holy Lamb of God,
On England's pleasant pastures seen!

And did the Countenance Divine,
Shine forth upon our clouded hills?
And was Jerusalem builded here,
Amongst these dark Satanic Mills?

Bring me my bow of burning gold:
Bring me my arrows of desire:
Bring me my Spear: O clouds unfold!
Bring me my Chariot of fire!

I will not cease from Mental Fight,
Nor shall my sword sleep in my hand:
Till we have built Jerusalem,
In England's green & pleasant Land.

Would to God that all the Lord's people were Prophets.
Number XI. Ch. 29 v."

-William Blake "Preface to Milton-

Prologue

It all began while I was searching for a photo of my great-grandad William Newbound feeding a goat.

To give you an idea of the sort of person he was, my great-grandad lived in a quarry house in Mansfield in north Nottinghamshire, just off Sheepbridge Lane along the River Maun and under the railway arches, in case you ever want to go there. He and my great-grandma had no electricity and drew their water from a well. Famously (in our family at least) when my grandma and grandad moved into their brand new 1950s bungalow up on Carter Lane with running water (very posh) and were discussing the cost of water rates, he said "Paying for water! You'll be paying for the bloody air you breathe next!" which always stuck with me. He knew which way the wind was blowing, my great-grandad.

He had been coming into my mind a lot recently, calling to me across the barrier between the living and the dead. I couldn't quite put my finger on why he was getting in touch; couldn't quite hear him properly, it wasn't a very good phone line. All I could think was that Fran and I have a wall in our living room where we frame and put up pictures of all our respective families (those still alive in colour, and those who have passed in black and white) and I hadn't put his picture up yet. So I went searching and on the shelf of photo albums (remember them?) I found one of those plastic wallets you used to use to put important documents in, full of photos. Memories of times I had forgotten, but which came back to me in vivid Fuji Technicolor, random images from various parts of my life all thrown together. Not digital images accessed via the Cloud at the press of a button; but actual physical photographs. Visceral, touchable and caressable memories preserved in the aspic of developing solutions. Photos of my daughter Eleanor growing up, my first wife Rachel, friends; some who drifted away, and some who stayed. Sepia images of ancestors heard of but never met. All jumbled together in that forgotten plastic wallet. What was important to me in this trip down memory lane, wasn't so much the images themselves; rather the stories that arose from each image as it revealed itself. It is as if viewing the photos woke the librarian in my head from a long slumber, jerking him awake from his drool-stained tome to pick up his round spectacles and go searching in the Akashic records for long lost treasure.

Among them were the photos you will find in the final section of this book; captured moments from two magical walks, one to Hartland in Devon, and the other to Bodmin in Cornwall, that Julian Vayne and I undertook soon after publishing *Now That's What I Call Chaos Magick Vol I & II* (let's abbreviate that to *NTWICCM* from now on). Looking back in my copy of the book it must have been 2005-2006. A good eleven years have passed between then and now. This passing of time is important because looking back in hindsight I am not so much remembering the actual events, as the *stories* I have told about the actual events. These stories subtly change with each telling, especially over the course of ten years, so the book you are reading is really how we both view those walks with the preferences and prejudices we both have now, in 2017.

In the plant medicine traditions of Central America, participants are given the opportunity to undertake a series of vision quests over four consecutive years. The first year (or First Door) is four days and nights alone on the mountain without food or water, within a 2 metre square surrounded by red thread and 365 tobacco prayers in small pouches. The second door is seven days, the third door eleven days, and the fourth door is thirteen days. In some traditions the participant is not allowed to talk about their vision for a year as the story starts to become the experience, and the story does not serve the teller, only the audience. We start to remember the story rather than the actual experience. Therefore, if we start telling stories of the experience we have no idea how the increasing and changing story memory of the experience will interfere with the psyche of the teller. This is a real dilemma when trying to communicate what the experience of these plants is to an audience that has no experience of what is being described.

So, telling the stories of these walks does not come without a risk to us, the tellers. In a way we have tried to circumnavigate this dilemma by waiting such a long time to tell the stories of the walks.

In the Amazon there still exists a tribe that believes we are walking backwards through our lives. The past is laid out before us, we can see it with memory; but the future is behind us, we are blind to it. It is unknowable and unseen. In a sense, we are viewing the walks we did through a ten-year telescope; they are far away in that landscape. Fragments that we glimpse as a series of 23 images, each one a frame in a graphic novel in which we have lost all the text: Leaving us to fill in the gaps with our memories and stories.

It is 2017 and culturally we are living in 'interesting times', politically we are entering a period of separation. Donald Trump has just been elected President of the USA, and the UK has just decided to leave the European Union. Along with this, science and technology is surpassing our ability to manage its implementation into the world. We can effect more and more change in the world with our leaps in AI, nanotech and genetics; but there is nobody capable of asking *if* we should. Albert Borgmann, in his seminal text on technology[1] way back in the 1980s, saw our move towards an increasingly technological world as one which moves towards 'dissociation' between ourselves and the world around us, this dissociation leading to increased isolation of the individual and disconnection from other people and the world outside of 'screen time'.

---

1. "Technology and the Character of Contemporary Life: A Philosophical Enquiry", Borgmann A.,1984

We are social beings, and this dissociation can be seen as leading to increased mental illness and deterioration of our physical, emotional and magical being. Therefore I am interested in promoting 'association' and 'associative' practices. Behaviours which connect us to the world around us, and each other. A coming together which encourages new contacts, deeper relationships and health.

Since undertaking these walks (and really since the work undertaken in *NTWICCM*) I have been involved in participatory art practices that associate people to Nature and each other. Planting and managing woodlands in the far west of Cornwall, teaching Wilderness living skills, green woodwork and traditional archery, taking people into the landscape and creating artwork with them. Practical activities that require people to join in and 'get their hands dirty'; slow down and associate themselves with what is happening around them. To touch, feel, hear, taste and see Nature as a beautiful living being that provides everything solid in our lives; from our bodies to our mobile phones. It all comes from Nature, and we cannot destroy or create anything she provides. All we can do is transform and manipulate her gifts, together with the energy of the Sun, to build other more complex or simple forms. The water, carbon and other elements are transformed through photosynthesis to create trees and plants, the decomposed bodies of ancient sea creatures are (among other uses) changed into petrol which we burn to create heat, light, noise and carbon dioxide (among other gases) which then gets released into the atmosphere. Nothing is destroyed, all is transformed.

To live on this planet there are few indisputable facts (particularly important in this Social Media 'Post Truth' world of competing narratives, see *NTWICCM*), but among them is that we need five things to survive on this planet; clean air to breathe, clean water to drink, healthy food to eat, fire to warm us and some sort of shelter to protect us from the elements. If one of these is taken away then sooner or later we will die. We can obtain these things ourselves direct from Nature if we have the knowledge to do so; or we can pay someone to supply them to us (government, water company, supermarket, energy supplier etc.). If we pay someone to supply them for us then we are reliant on a faceless corporate/governmental entity for our survival, locked into a toxic parental-child relationship with it. We become dis-empowered to live independently, with the accompanying baseline anxiety associated with the feeling that "if I don't have a job then I can't pay for them and I, and my family, will die". We become increasingly distanced from the freedom and heritage our ancestors passed to us, and the Natural world on which we rely. Learning Wilderness Living skills provides you with the ability to obtain these things for yourself from Nature. It's not that you will purify your own drinking water from a stream, or chop your own wood every day; but that you have the *ability* to do these things if needed. Invariably, you also find that obtaining these things for yourself, even occasionally, ensures you befriend Nature and your surroundings, deepens your relationship with the World and frees you from anxiety and fear. Every man, woman and child on this Earth should know how to get these five basic things for themselves before they pick up a mobile phone or log onto the Web, because they bring freedom.

The process of learning these skills requires us to participate in Nature, we cannot learn these skills from a book or TV documentary. Nature likes us to be with her. For this book to work you are required to participate. Use it as a guide to visit the places it describes or go on your own magical walks, your own magical pilgrimages to Hartland and Roughtor, to places dear to you. By travelling in this conscious way you 'associate' yourself with the landscape you are walking in. I urge you to go and weave your own tales and stories while you travel on your own magical walks in places that have some significance for you.

"This is Old Magic. This is the magic in the old folk tales and myths. Magic passed down by Word of Mouth."

By telling stories about places, and by fixing these stories to particular geographical locations, we create mythological associations for them. This mythologisation of landscape is important because it makes these places special, it creates a connection between the land we experience outside ourselves and our *inner* landscape, which is the realm of your mental, emotional and spiritual bodies. You are only as healthy as your inner landscape, so be aware of how you are feeding it. I like to call this dynamic exploration of inner and outer territory 'psychogeography'.

There is a powerful link between the inner landscape and the landscape we normally consider as being 'outside'. They reflect each other with the inner landscape being composed of the things you pay attention to in the outer. In the 'normal', outer, waking world we decide where to place our attention and awareness and this then has an influence on our inner landscape (e.g. watching a lot of pornography will mean sex plays a larger role in our imaginatively constructed world). This is not a one-way street however, and as well as the outer world affecting the inner, the inner can also affect the outer. The imaginative landscape can affect our mood, which is the coloured lens through which we then experience the world outside of ourselves. This can have an affect like a ripple on a pond, spreading out into the world; thus demonstrating the barrier between the worlds is actually a permeable membrane, rather than a hard and fixed boundary. To take a simple example, if I wake on a Sunday morning from a great dream, feeling good, relaxed and at peace with the world, I carry on my day, visit the supermarket and share a smile and a jokey conversation with Mike who works behind the till. He then feels better about his day and passes that on to all the people he meets in the course of his job. Such sequences influence how we see the world outside, and consequently our actions within it.

"As Above, so Below."

This is everyday magick in action, and isn't really shocking or revelatory; but the knowledge of this magick brings a responsibility. All you can do as a magician is change your own inner landscape; through this you change your mood, words and actions that in turn affects the world. Conjure the world you want to live in.

In England we have a tradition of applying this thought process to landscape. Our folk tales and myths are stories we tell each other about real places, actual physical locations in the landscape.

They are the vehicle we use to link the inner and outer landscapes, and through them a bond is created between the landscape we walk through with our feet, and the one we journey through in our minds. This storytelling tradition is a sacred magick that joins us to the land and the more tales we tell, the more the relationship deepens. The stories we tell about places anchor those places in our inner world; and create a shared mythological world on top of our own personal myth.

This collective mythological landscape is called 'Albion', where we build the world of the Lost Gods once again and its body is constructed from the tales we tell of the places that exist. Folk tales and mythological cycles based in actual places are its flesh and bones; this Otherworld that exists and overlays the land we see every day. It is just a hair's breadth away and all we need is a shift of perception to see it. Weave your own tales, create associations and enrich your inner landscape. In this way Albion becomes alive once more. The sleeper awakens, and together we can build a mythical Jerusalem in England's green and pleasant land.

The Walks

Hartland

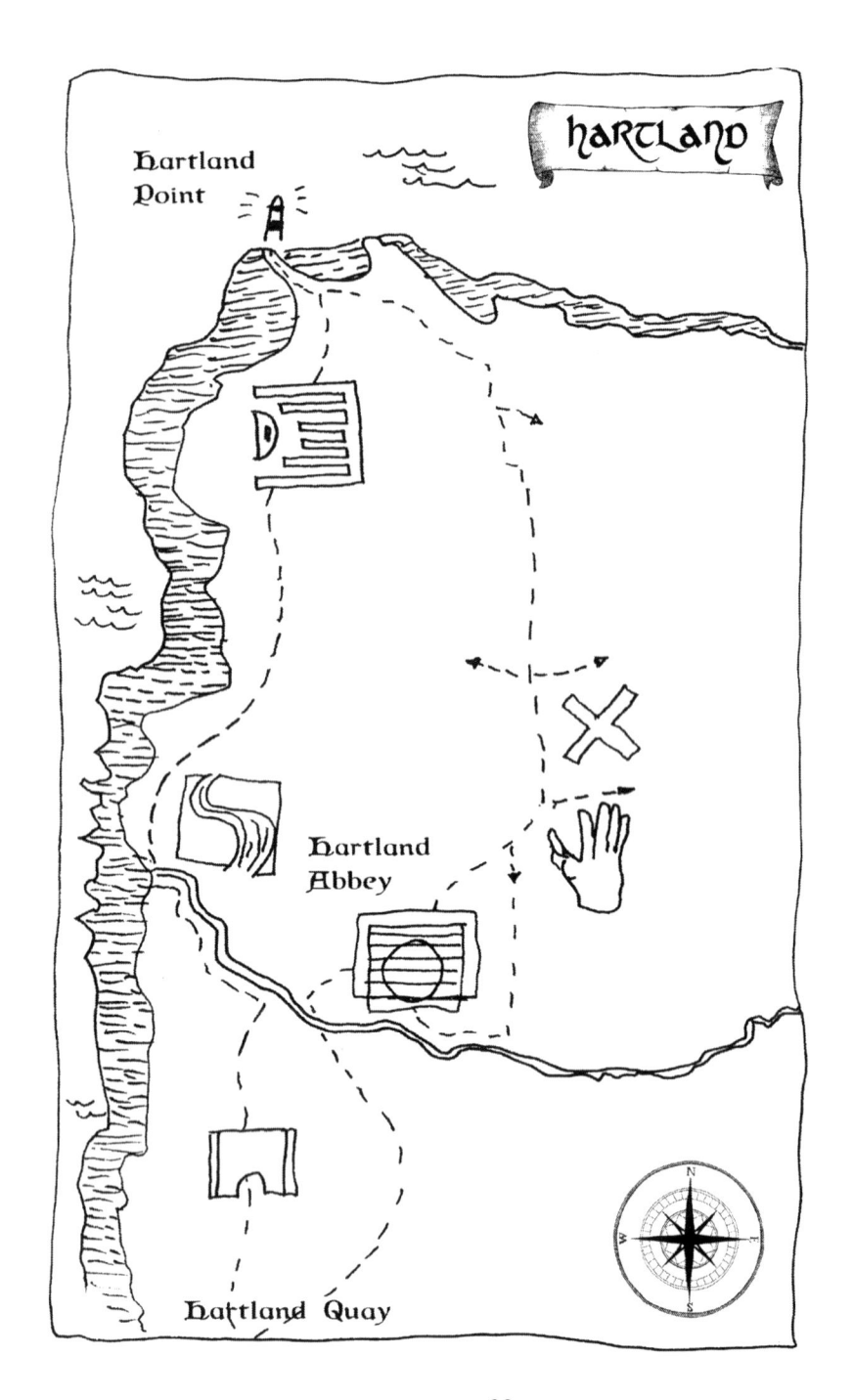

Hartland Point

Hartland Abbey

Hartland Quay

HARTLAND POINT

I remember we chose the locations of the walks randomly. Placing a pencil into the map between our homes in Devon and Cornwall. Hartland and Roughtor were the places that came up as if they were gifts descending from the ocean of the Otherworld to become manifest in this world. Playgrounds for us to walk between the worlds, to explore and understand more about ourselves and the Land. Landscapes for us to tell stories about.

At Hartland Point there is an arch on the cliff. Looking West over the Atlantic Ocean one way, and East towards Bideford and the rest of Southern England. A portal facing two ways at the same time; a geographical Janus. This is the start of our journey and we like to leave offerings at the beginning of any pilgrimage. We have brought a selection of magical objects from our respective homes; art materials, cups, woollen thread, old dress jewellery, coins, chocolate and sacred herbs. Creating an altar immediately makes a place special, and generally people who follow tend to respect it as a place of the spirit. People tend to add to these altars if they are created with care and an intent to make a place more beautiful. They grow.

We say what needs to be said and we make our way North. Dropping down to a stream which runs West to the sea. Flat stones of granite line the bed of the running water and dry rocks break the water's surface to create stepping stones. Charcoal and chalk come out to mark this place as special. Swirls and lines reflect the patterns in the water's surface as it bubbles and babbles past us towards its lowest point. Back to its Mother, the Ocean.

As we walk along the stream to its source, and its ending, I am drawn to a piece of driftwood. It must have been a root at one time, but now is something quite different. Bleached white and smooth as a baby's skin it is perhaps 3-feet long with a sharp right angle at its base. A spirit stick given as a gift and a spell. A spell to communicate the spirit world to the human world.

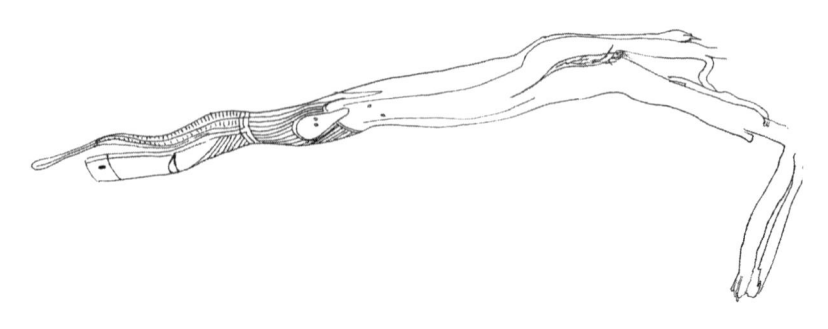

We arrive on the pebble and stone-strewn beach. Facing the Ocean and the Western Wind, the two spirits that make the waves and refresh the soul. We gather stones and balance them to make precarious towers. Liminal and temporary artworks to celebrate the sea and its grinding, abrasive beauty. We bathe, and wash ourselves in the cold, salty brine. The smell of purest ozone filling our lungs as the water replenishes our skin. A bone-deep feeling of renewal and rejuvenation. The embrace of Mother Ocean, the deepest hug.

Then dressing and up the cliff. The generated heat of our own bodies drying them as we ascend; and with it a deep feeling of relaxation and vitality. Further we climb, blood returning to extremities to pump life back into toes and fingers. Breathing hard, feeling the ache and burn of life in muscles and skin. Taking care of each step upon the path we look down, keeping our own counsel we look within. The discomfort forcing to the surface our own shadows, bringing the hidden into the light. Unbidden the difficult memories and thoughts arise, they are witnessed and cannot be ignored.

At last the summit is reached. The body and spirits laid to rest upon the soft, green Earth. All can be given to the Earth; the shadows and the pain. She transforms all into beautiful growing things. The plants, the trees, the birds, the animals, the stones, the metals, the material world all arises from Her. Viva Pachamama!

We share a moment of clarity lying face up amongst the yarrow, facing a grey cloudy sky skittering from the Western Ocean. The sheer cliffs march away to the South and I draw what I see before me using chalk on a rock. From our perch on the cliff edge we can see to the North, the way forward. Below the cliff on a low vulnerable promontory stands the white tower of Hartland Point lighthouse. The light in the night, warning of danger and comforting at the same time. Guiding our way onwards.

Moving towards the Point we come across a place that was not on any map. A chain-link fence walks with us next to the path, and I can't decide if the fence is there to keep us out, or whatever lives there in. We make another shrine at this place by twining wool, hanging jewellery and weaving flowers into the wire fence, its diamond shaped squares acting like small picture frames and the whole thing reminding me of the similar act of magic performed by the women at Greenham Common. We want to make this place more beautiful than when we found it. There is no photo of this place. This place does not exist.

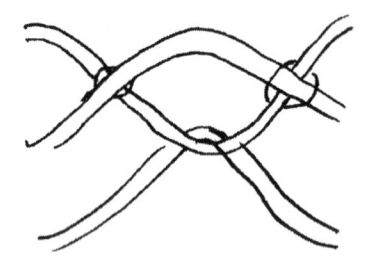

Onwards we go, to where our feet will take us. And our feet take us to the café for a proper Devon Cream tea. Gorgeous.

Next we move inland. On tracks and metalled roads. Quiet single track roads creating a sunken maze with no vantage point to see the whole. Junctions and signposts pointing in every direction. The Crossroads is reached. The place of Exu, and the trickster Gods. Blues musicians were said to go to the Crossroads if they wanted success; but there is always a price to be paid. The devil gives you options and from a single-pointed place of peace where there is only one way there forms a question. 'Which way shall I go?" Doubt rises like a bubble from the depths. "Which is the right way?" We decorate the cross at the crossroads with a mermaid, colours and charms. An offering to Exu for his work in showing us who we are.

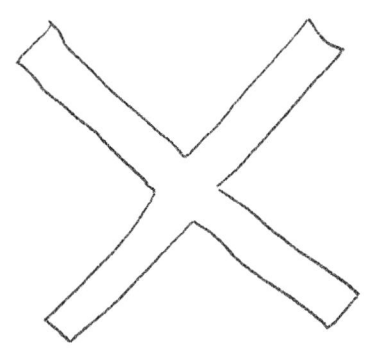

We travel until we reach an empty piece of hardboard tacked to a telegraph post. The perfect opportunity to make our mark. If I told you I took the sacred blade and cut my palm, letting the blood pool in my cupped fingers then coating my hand with it before planting it in the middle of the board. A handprint in blood. If I told you that, would you believe me? If I told you I sang the songs of sacrifice, would you even question that they exist? Would you care? Sometimes you have to give something that really matters to you before you can find the answer you are looking for.

The indigenous people of remote parts of Brazil, Mexico and Peru believe sacrifice to the Earth (Pachamama) is essential for establishing harmony with it. Animals that have often been living with, and cared for by the families involved are brought into the ceremonial space. They are stroked and calmed as the ceremony progresses, until they lie down peacefully of their own volition. They are then sung to, and prayed for, and thanked before they are swiftly killed with a knife. Their blood is given to the earth, some of the meat is given to the Fire, some to the Ancestors and the rest to the people. The Waririka of Central Mexico travel each year from the mountains where they live across the desert to the sacred mountain Wirikuta. This is where the peyote grow, the place of the Blue Deer spirit. Along the way of their pilgrimage they leave sacrifices at sacred places, thanking the nature spirits and saying prayers for us all. The idea of sacrifice is a tricky one for me and my cultural background. At what point does a sacrifice become unacceptable? Chocolate? Flowers? Fruit? Tobacco? Money? Time? Precious jewels? Our own blood? Fish? Animals? Willing humans? Unwilling humans? Children? And what criteria are we applying to that decision? Which of our inner voices is talking to us when we decide this?

You see how Exu shows us who we are.

We come to a stream crossing our path. Flat stones stand a few centimetres proud of the waters' surface. A stepping stone bridge across the river. Three stones stand apart from the others. The charcoal colours them black and the chalk swirls, mirroring the sunlight reflected in the brook's surface. Tiny rainbows form in the corners of my eyes as we cross the sacred waters to the 'other side'.

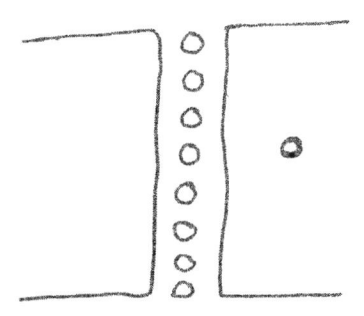

I remember a silver chord emerging from my belly button and moving ahead of me up the hills. It pulls me forward and the climb is much easier; and in no time at all we have arrived. The spring stands before us, locked in its little stone house. The Well of St Nectan, a 6th-century hermit who was killed by robbers who cut off his head. After his decapitation, Nectan promptly picked up his head and brought it here, leaving it hidden to perform miracles while the rest of him ascended Upstairs.

The head is seen as the seat of the soul in many cultures, past and present. Tacitus relates that the Druids used to carry the heads of their enemies on their belts, which makes more sense to me after hearing the following tale. The tribes in South America that hunt heads do so to help heal the souls of those they have killed.

The heads are only taken from enemies that have sworn to harm the family of the hunter. The enemy is killed and then the head is taken and it is skinned, sewn and preserved over several days. All that time the hunter is singing songs and saying prayers for the soul of his enemy, helping heal it and transforming all the anger and hate the enemy had for the hunter and his family into love and light. The hunter becomes the soul midwife for the person they have hunted. Helping them on their journey to the Otherworld. Thank you for helping us on our journey, St Nectan!

And then we return. A short walk over many-tracked long grass to the portal where we began our journey. We sing songs and give prayers of thanks to all the spirits that have guided and helped us on our journey. We step over the threshold and back to this life. Somewhere in the back of our minds we must have retained the knowledge the journey gave us; somewhere lying dormant for the right time to emerge into the world.

Albion Awake!

"There's a feeling I get
When I look to the west,
And my spirit is crying for leaving.
In my thoughts I have seen
Rings of smoke through the trees,
And the voices of those who stand looking."
- Stairway to Heaven, Led Zeppelin

Once there were two brothers; one from the North and one from the South who wished to create a great magic. An old magic, that would help the people with their problems and troubles.

"Let's go and see the Gods about it, see if they can help?", they said. They had heard of a place called Hartland which contained a Portal to the Otherworld. So in time, they travelled together. On a cliff high above the Western Ocean, there it stood. The Doorway.

42

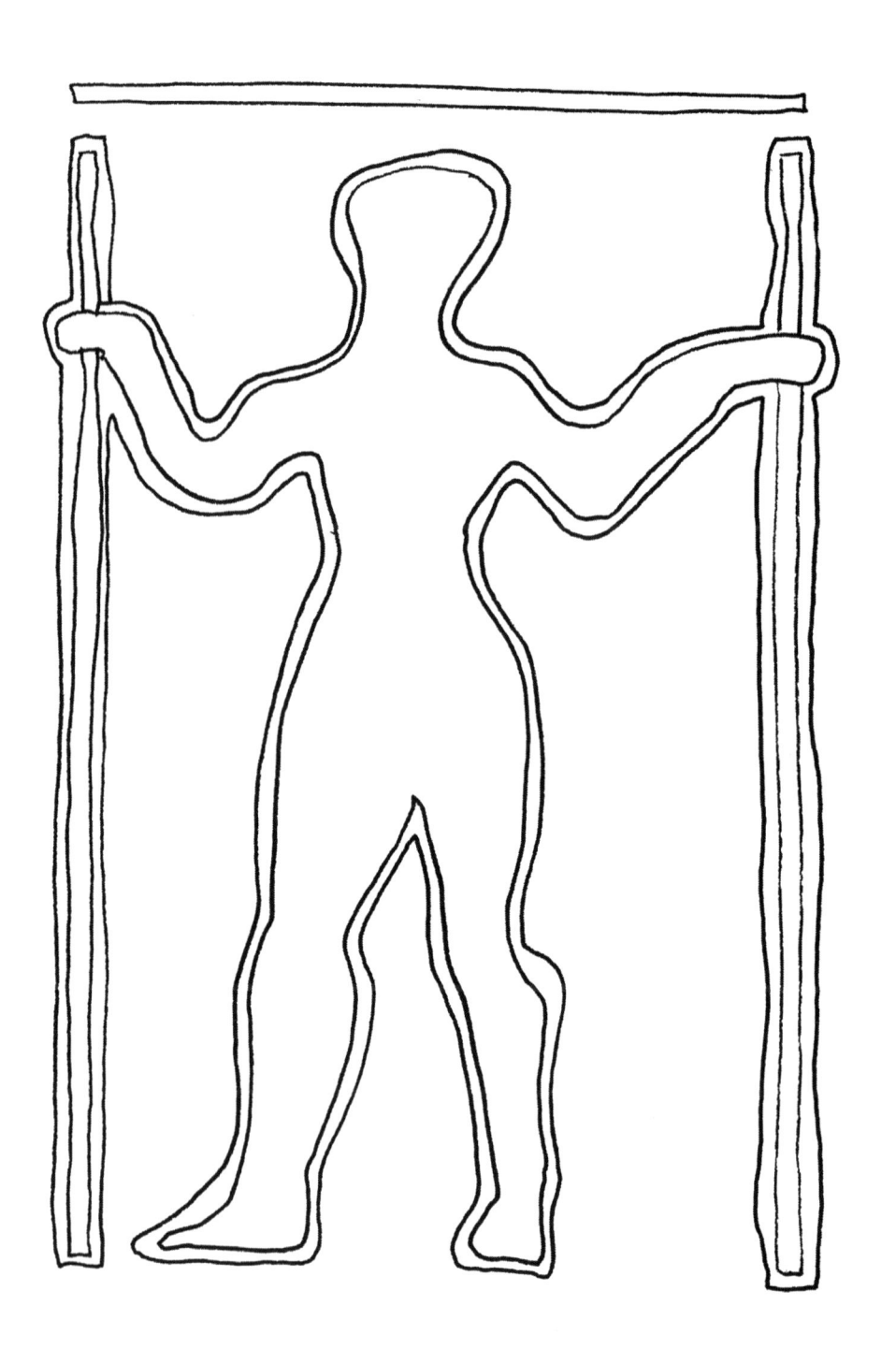

This Doorway was warded by a God called Wendel. Standing with his arms outstretched guarding the frame, barring the way. The brothers approached and laid, on an altar at his feet, offerings as a way to remind themselves that they were more than their physical bodies. To free their spirits, which rose up and walked towards Wendel who moved aside and opened the door for them.

44

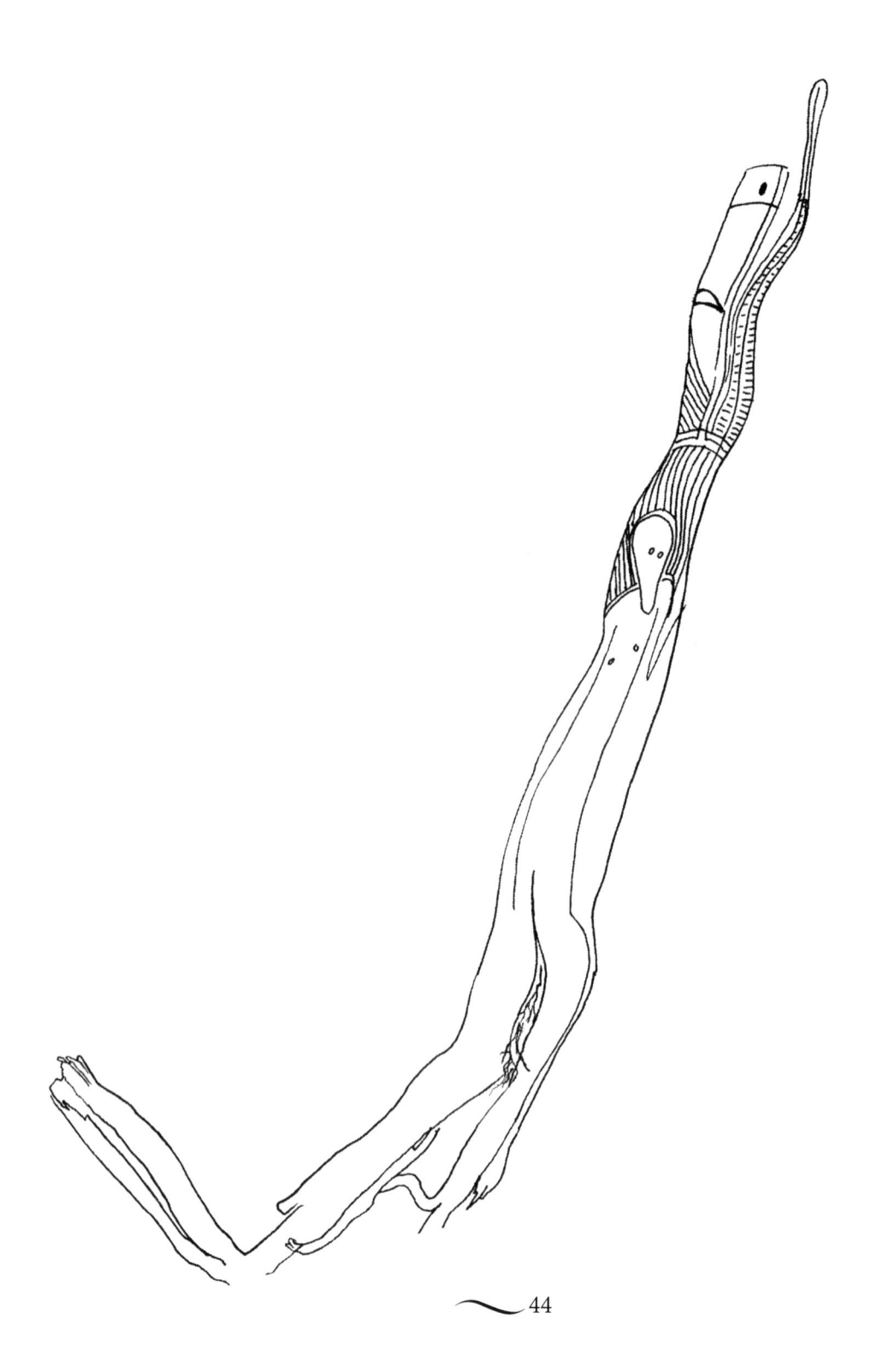

Over the threshold they passed and down the green hill across the land to where they could see laid in the bottom of a valley a silver snake-like dragon. Glistening and shimmering in the sun, its body writhing and trailing behind its head.

"How do we find our Mother? We are lost and need your help, O beautiful shining one", they pleaded.
"Climb on my back and I'll take you to her", said the dragon in reply. They climbed up, and down to the ocean the dragon and the two brothers went. When they arrived the dragon called far out to the Western horizon. A haunting call of separation, which then grew into one of merging and reunion.

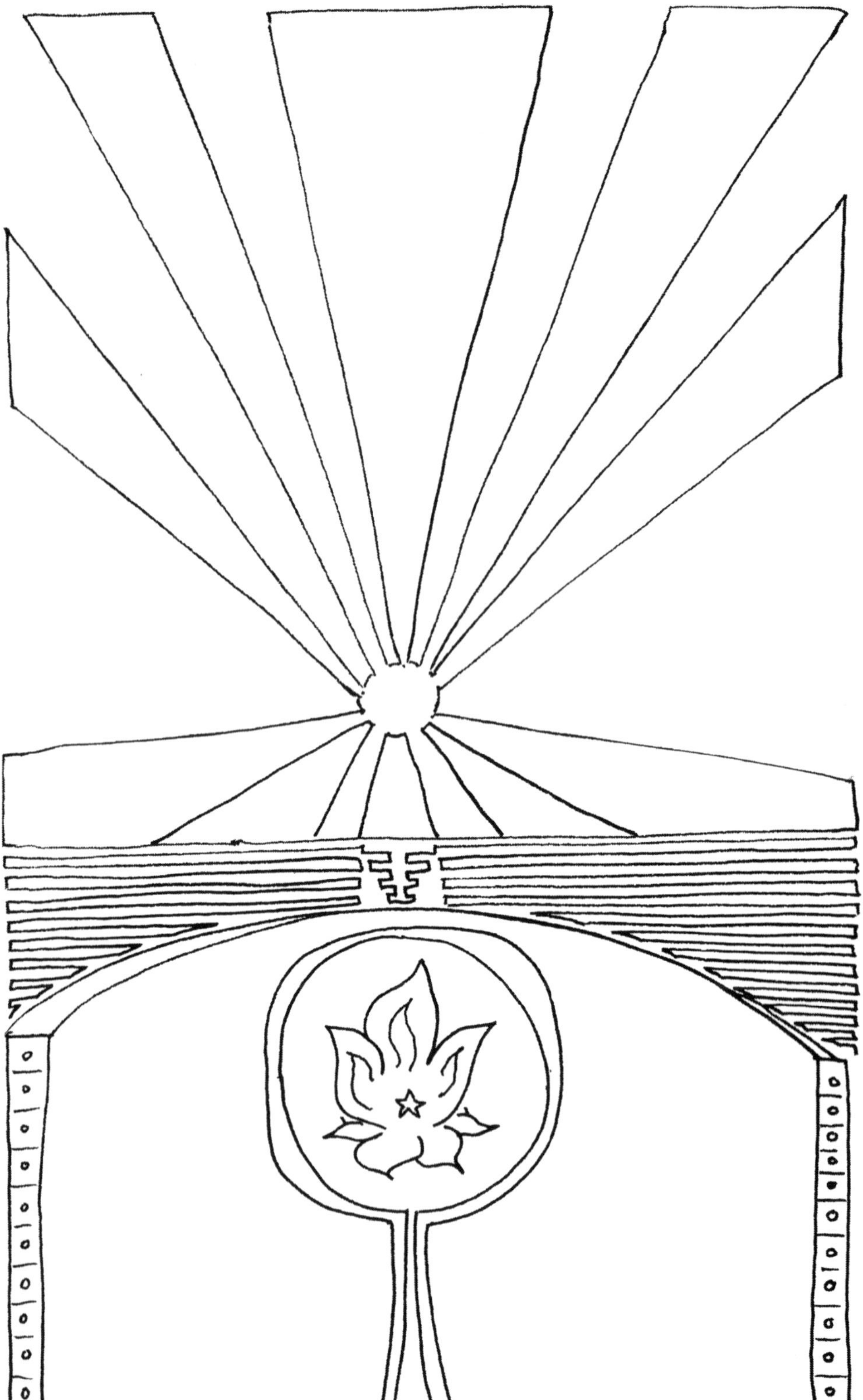

And she came. The Mother, as a Star of the Wave, rose above the horizon and said to them:

"My sons, look to the West. What do you see?"

"The Otherworld", they replied in unison

"but what is it like over there? We need to tell the people what it is like to help ease their troubles."

"It is pointless to try and describe the experience of the Otherworld. All you can do is describe your journey to get there. The journey can be the footsteps of forgotten souls, or shine as a bright new penny. This is what the spirits told me to tell you."

The brothers thanked her, staring into her shimmering light. The bright waves of her starlight moved through them, and they moved towards her presence shining before them. Over the waves they moved towards the light in the gathering darkness, soaring on wings of shining light. Beautiful birds gliding over the Ocean.

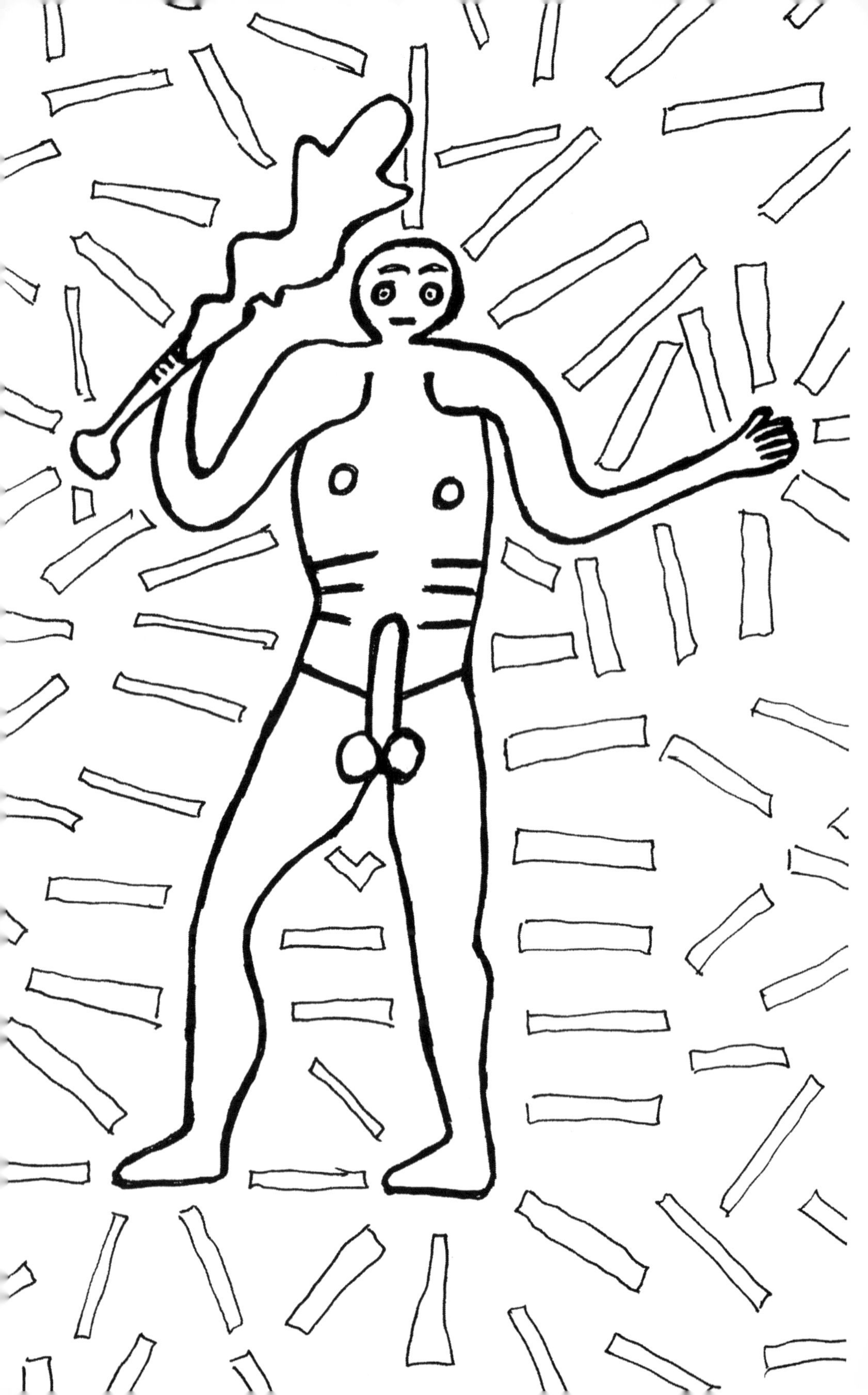

And suddenly their way was barred. A fearsome giant rose before them, club raised high in the air; cock rigid, inflamed and angry. The brothers held their distance and called;

"We are sorry if we have offended you O giant; but what can we do to pass through your lands?"

The giant stood on the spot, screaming at them, raging and shaking his huge club at them, gobbets of spittle shooting from his clenched teeth. When the brothers moved to the left, so did the giant; when they moved right, so did the giant; and when they moved forward, so did the giant. So the brothers stopped. Paused. Then began to lay objects of precious metals and cloth of bright colours in front of him as he furied. They sang songs to the spirits, that they may come and help the giant find the place where he would be content, at peace. Then they waited. And slowly out of the West it came. Trotting on Golden hooves, a snow white lamb; jumping occasionally and shaking its tail. Beside it, in a clear blue sky, fluttering in the breeze was the pennant of a red cross on a white background.

The brothers sat and watched in a field of lush green grass, looking upwards to the beech copse crowned hill, as the lamb gambolled over to the giant who promptly put down his club and followed it through the meadow flowers and butterflies. To the light, to the West. Into the light until they were tiny specks against its blazing glory ... and then gone.

As the star, the guide whose path towards which our Brothers were travelling, set in the West, they saw it slowly pull apart, separating into two separate stars. The stars continued to move out, separating into the constellations we see in a clear dark sky.

"Now which star are you going to choose to follow? Which one is your path?" a voice whispered.

Indecision, doubt and uncertainty assailed our Brothers at the crossroads. Flying on their wings of light. "We don't know which star to follow, and are asking for help", the brothers asked the stars before them. "Please help us, O stars, guide us to the Otherworld that we might bring something back home that will help the people with their troubles!"

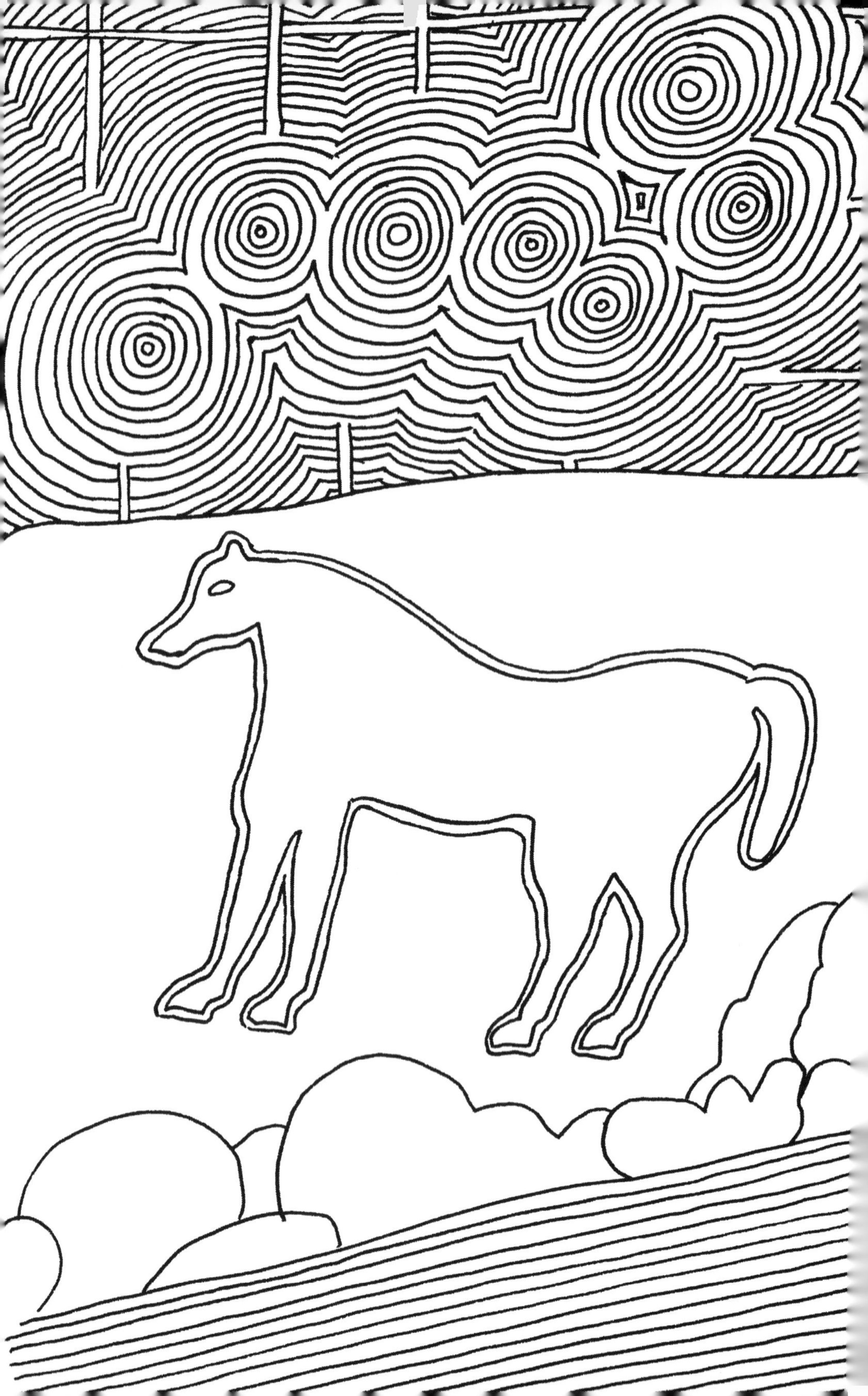

The stars heard them, and one of the stars reached out to them. A rainbow bridge glowing in pink, yellow, and green; blue, orange and violet it appeared at their feet, stretching away to the second star on the right. They set their feet upon it and began walking, marvelling at the colours and patterns all about them. It was a long time before the brothers could travel no more, tired of their exploring the seemingly endless multitude of beauty about them. But no matter how entrancing the scene might be, there came a time when they needed to rest. So they lay down together where they had stood amongst the rainbows.

The noise they heard first; the clip-clop of the pale horse walking towards them. It halted by the pair and waited for them to rise and climb on its back; then continued on its way, sure and steady.

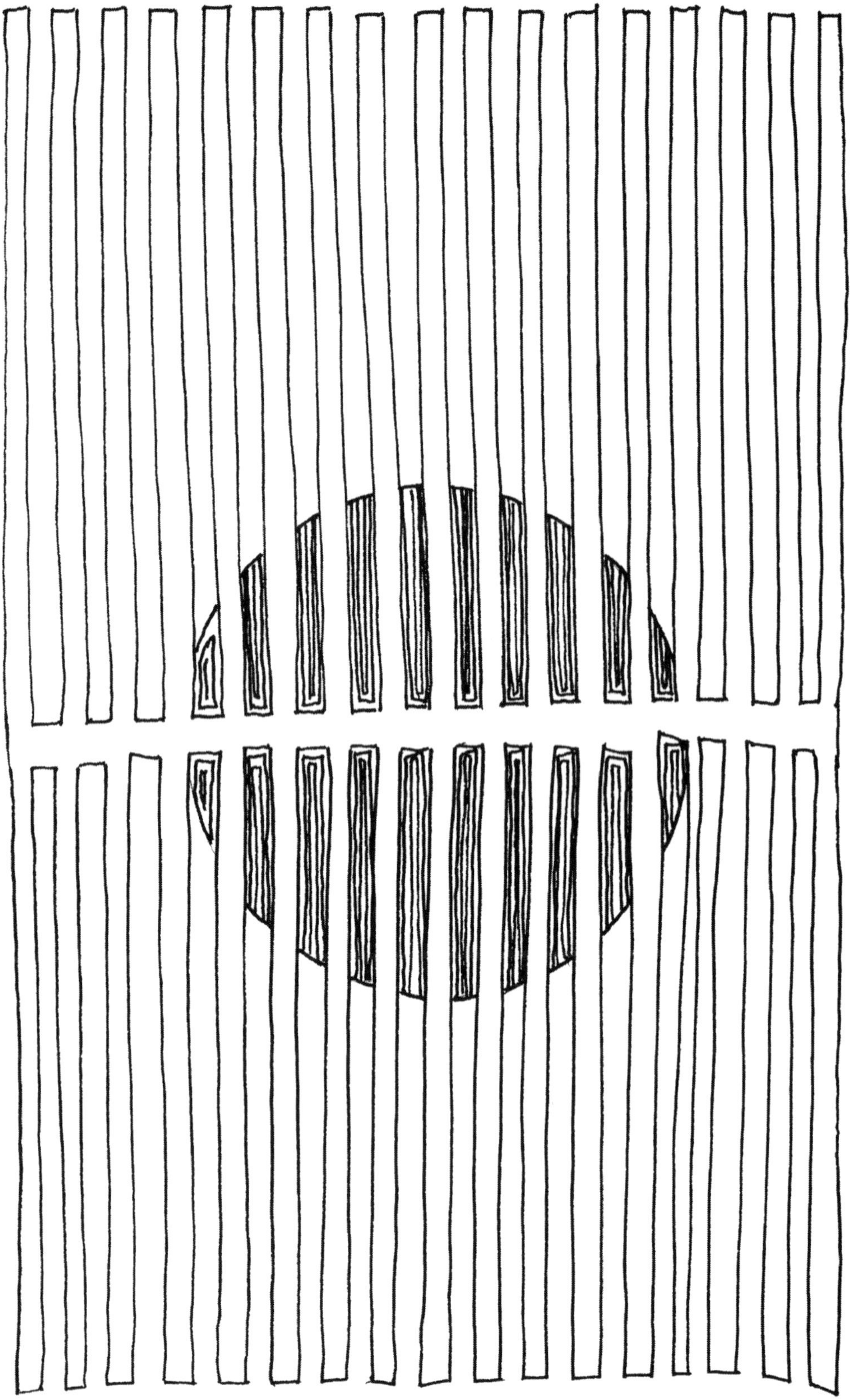

It carried them all the way to a clearing in the woods on the far side of the rainbow bridge. In the centre of the clearing stood a well, with a wooden cup placed on its rim. The brothers walked to the well's edge and peered through the crystal clear water into its unfathomable depths. In turn they dipped the cup into the water and drank deep of the water.

"Will we remember this when we get back home?", asked one brother.

"If you tell the people what you found", replied the water.

So now I have told you what we found, and my tale is told.

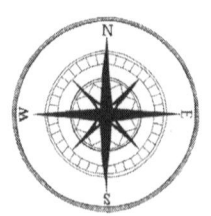

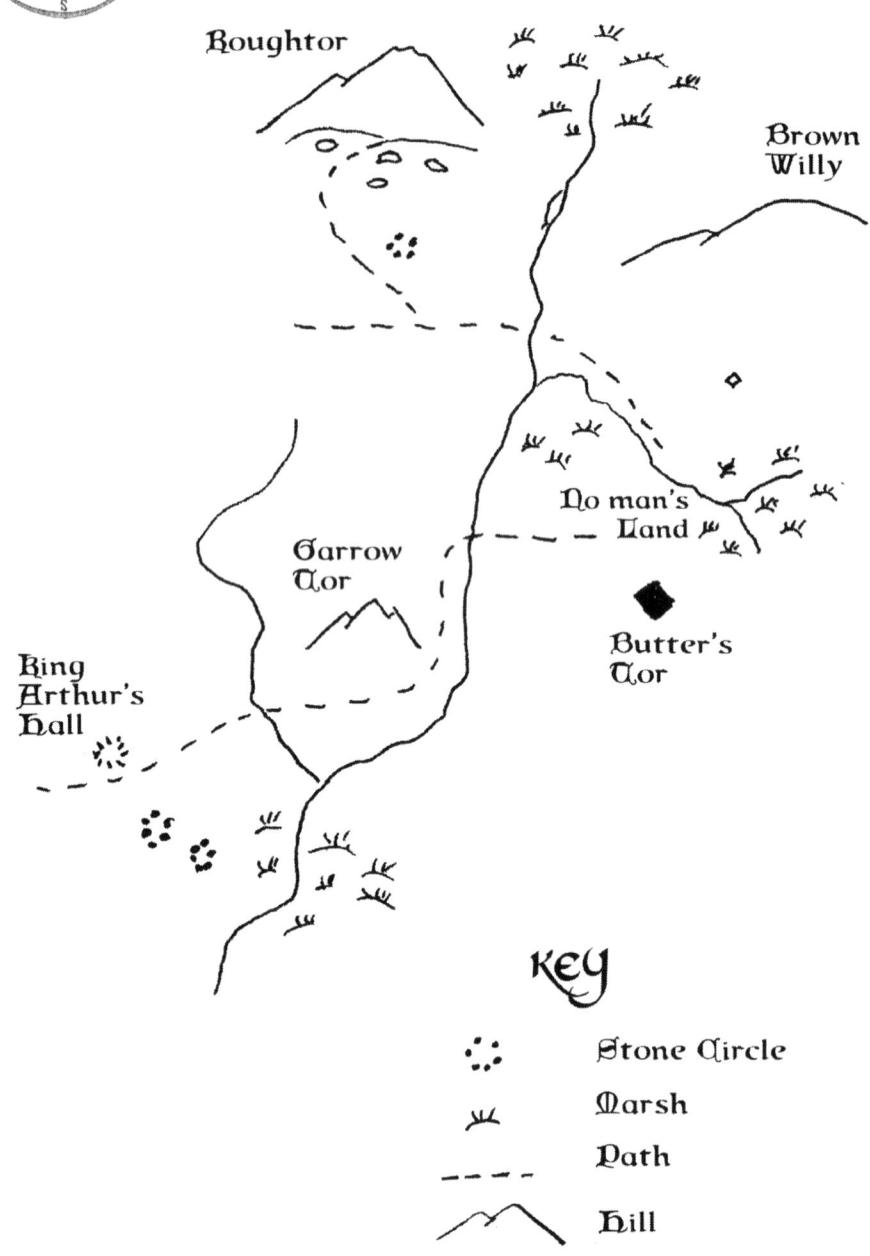

ROUGHTOR

Roughtor

Brown Willy

No man's Land

Garrow Tor

Butter's Tor

King Arthur's Hall

KEY

- Stone Circle
- Marsh
- Path
- Hill

ROUGHTOR

I love treasure hunts! The travelling and exploring of landscape to reveal treasure. One Easter, Joolz was down at my place and our children were pre-teens so we decided to set them an egg hunt, not around the house (which was our usual thing) but around the local neighbourhood. We told the kids that they should get up early for the Easter Egg hunt as we had placed their chocolate eggs in the local area with clues leading one from the other. Now I live next to a moorland, with a beacon hill just behind the house, a local Holy Well, woods and an Iron Age hill fort close by. Our children packed rucksacks with torches, a flask of hot chocolate and snacks; left just as the Sun rose and were back before breakfast. Even now, years later they still remember that morning and that landscape they entered. From simple Easter Egg hunts we set for the children, to the complex puzzles of Kit Williams' excellent *Masquerade*[1]; I love them all. So we decided to set one ourselves.

---

1. A cultural phenomenon in the 1970s. The artist Kit Williams made a golden, jeweled hare and encased it in a bespoke clay pot. which he buried in the English Countryside. The beautiful book *Masquerade* contained the solution to where he had buried the hare and people bought the book and spent weekends chasing over the countryside trying to find it.

Song For The Dead

Roughtor has always been a place sacred to the ancestors, and various communities from the Iron Age to the Saxon left objects and their dead there. The craggy Tor itself was never wooded and would have risen high above the oak and hazel woods surrounding it on Bodmin Moor.

The boundary to this walk lay between the town and the wilderness. We realised it had been reached when the last dwelling was passed. In front of you lies The Wild. By a stream we pause and perform some Tai Chi exercises, quelling the eagerness and desire to get going. Then the single-pointed consciousness of the mushroom hunt. Head down looking about 3ft in front of your feet for the small plant allies that grow and exist in this place. The focus is similar when we walk up the hills, our gaze settles in front of our feet and our thoughts turn inward towards our selves. Towards the Underworld.

We placed a bodhran (Irish drum) I had played in several crusty, punk inspired folk bands in the early 1990s (a whole other story, believe me!), in King Arthur's Hall (SW 129777) by the ancient settlement at the foot of Roughtor. We could actually see it by ignoring the map, letting our curiosity of the features we can actually see around us be our guide.

"Wood for the living, stones for the Dead", that's what they say.

Anyway, we left this drum in the remote King Arthur's Hall in a waterproof case, I took a picture with a polaroid camera of Joolz

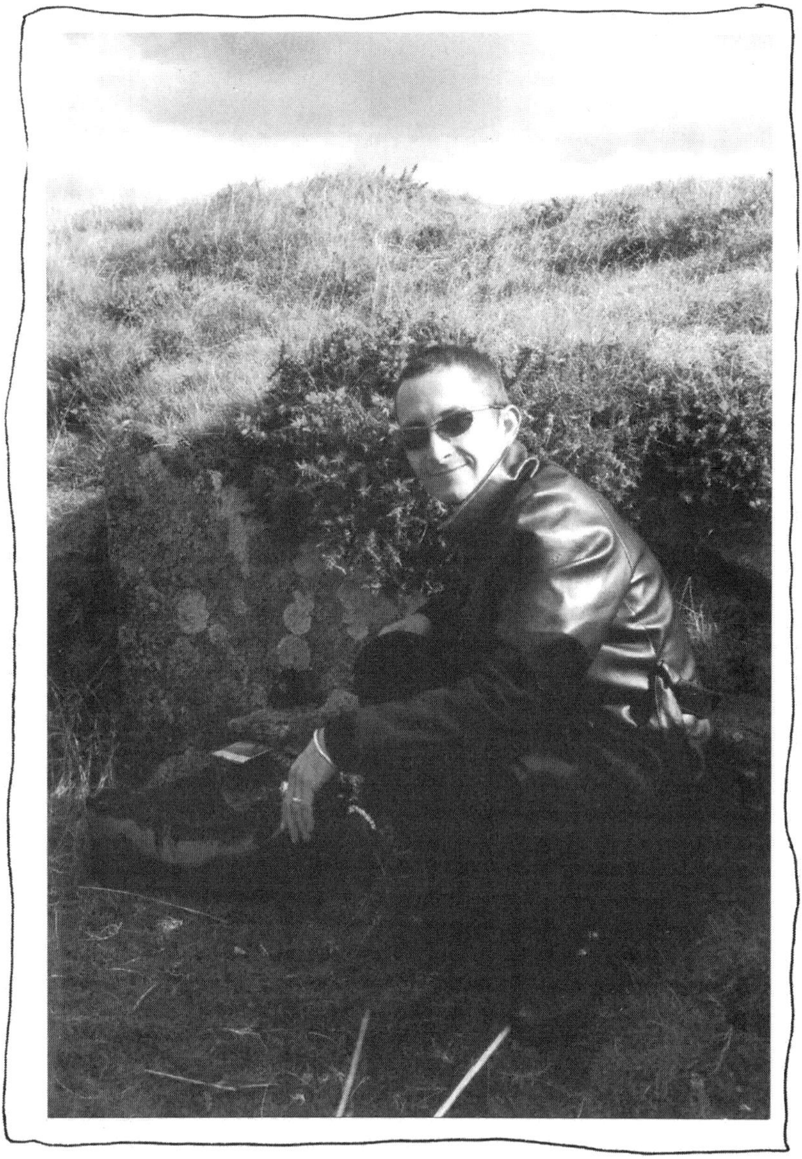

pointing to Roughtor, and stuck it onto the drum case so people could see it.

Then we started walking to Roughtor. The path led through small patches of woodland, and mushrooms lay before us in the close cropped grasses of the moorland fields. We walked in an easy, relaxed way. Plenty of time for us to enjoy being in this place and listening to it.

The stone circle brooded in the sunny expanse of the close cropped grass of the moor. I stood against the stones letting its monolithic bulk take my weight as I sank into it. Melting into it. Dissolving.

By the fir woods, further down the path ran a gloriously lush and clear stream. On its bank sat the Guardian of the Path. We greeted him and he told us he had been sleeping on the banks of the stream for the night, with only a few mushrooms for company. He smiles, and we walk on receiving his silent permission.

There was always going to be a point where the path ran out. I'd seen it earlier on the OS map; but assumed we would find a way through somehow. It's only a gap about 400m long. The path ends, but we can see a track two fields over, which will take us to the foot of the Tor. The problem is the barbed wire and electric fence combination directly in front of us barring our path. Having no desire to walk to the right towards the farmhouse (they obviously don't want visitors!) I decide we should try and go around the fence to the left. And as expected the fence does turn in the desired direction. Straight through a bog. Now, I have some experience of bogland up in the Derbyshire Peak District where the grassy tufts are solid enough and you can, with relative ease, hop from one to the other across wide, waterlogged areas. So with a cheery wave I say "Follow Me!" and jump onto the first grassy tuft, which promptly sinks below the water's surface. Too late I realise this 'grassy knoll' is actually only six inches deep and floating on the surface of a deep pool. My rucksack and I disappear below the peaty water, and I need my companion to pull me out onto the solid earth and the sunshine.

We really don't have any choice, to continue to Roughtor we have to cross the fence. So we retrace our steps and decide to climb the barbed wire and electric fence at a suitable point that would cause least damage. A fence post sits in front of a line of trees with a brace at 45 degrees. It is the brace we decide to place our feet on to traverse this obstacle. My companion climbs first, dextrously placing a foot on the brace then lifting his leg over the electric fence and jumping over. I attempt the same manoeuvre, but as I lift my leg over the electric fence my wet boot slips on the brace and my testicles descend onto the electrified wire. A curiously painful pulse of electricity is forced through my body via my scrotal sack, and another, and yet another, before I can extricate myself from the infernal thing.

We are now in uncharted territory, and we definitely feel we should not be here. All we have to do is to follow the line of trees to the track 400 metres away and then we can relax. The sound of an approaching engine forces us into a fight or flight response of fear. We both run, and hide behind the trees. Our response reminds me of rabbit medicine. Everything in the woodland wants to eat the rabbit, so it has to be cleverer, faster and sexually more abundant than all the opposition. We hide like frightened children until the quad bike goes past.

How does one cope with such a situation?

Of course, we fashion a rune stick using a pocket knife! Creating a bind rune for the spirits in this place. Calling them to us and through carving signs into the wood, the dead body of a tree, we direct their focus and power. The skill of our ancestors working through our hands, eyes and fingers. Connecting us to them through the physical activity of cutting. What we do, our ancestors did a hundred? a thousand? a million? times before us.

We then place this rune stick among the fir trees and build a "Xmas Tree" shrine for all the Christmas trees, and animistic spirits killed then thrown away. Wasted. As well as the rune stick, we place fir cones, wool and a cow thigh bone we had inscribed with the words "Merry Xmas".

X = Gyfu, joy through giving away, letting go, of anything that is no longer needed.

ᛡ = Jera, turning or changing. This too shall pass.

ᚱ = Raido, journeying and travel away from home.

We say our respective prayers at the shrine then make our cautious way towards the track and Roughtor itself.

As we get to the track we see a shielded area with the remains of burnt plastic and animal remains. It reminds me of the burnt corpses of cattle after the 2001 outbreak of Foot and Mouth disease. The smell is what I remember most. It reminds me of the smell we experienced looking over the river at the ghats in Khatmandu. Watching the bodies of the dead be burnt on pyres, then the ashen remains swept into the sacred water. Roast pork and burnt hair.

The stone circle at the base of the Tor became a station on the path for us to breathe again. Lay down, relax and wring out our socks and clothes.

After a stony climb we arrive on the summit of Roughtor, ears pounding and heart racing.

Looking over the magnificently wild and barren landscape back to King Arthur's Hall we took another Polaroid of Joolz pointing to King Arthur's Hall from here, and hung it as the final image on a string of prayer flags I had made at home.

The prayer flags read from left to right and began with a ...

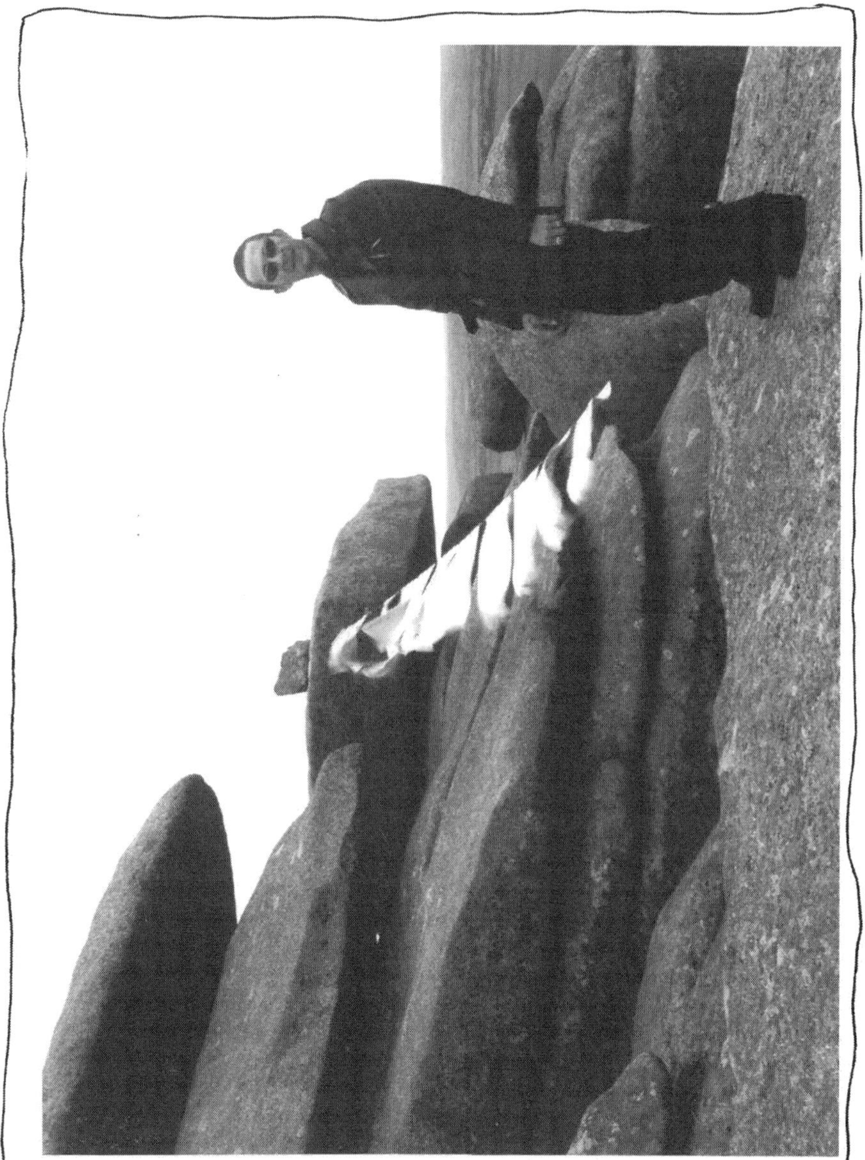

... Treasure Hunt -

"Here Lies the prize for solving the riddle,
A voice it has, but has no mouth,
And once acquainted will even sing.

(X marks the spot)

And leave another gift in its place,
For a friend you may not have met yet,
And be blessed, else be left in torment"

In between these two book-end images on the flags snapping in the wind, there then followed a series of images making a story map of my inner journey to this place, at this time. Roughtor 6th October 2010. This place of the ancestors where I ask the wind to take the news of my path to the silent ones who have gone before. A story for the Dead. In the peyote tradition the Red road is seen as the path of the living, the path of blood; and the Blue Road is the spirit road, the road of the Soul, the road of the Dead.

This is a Blue Road story; a prayer for healing the troubles of those who have gone before us, those who survived so each one of us could exist. Our ancestors.

Lies the prize for solving the
 Riddle.
A voice it has, but has no
 Mouth.
And once aquainted, it will
 Even Sing.

("X" marks the spot).

And leave another gift in
 its place.
For a friend you may not have
 Met yet.
And be blessed, else be left
 To Torment.

Story Map of the Hartland Walk - There are plan maps and there are story maps. Plan maps are the abstract 'bird's eye' view grids upon which we can locate specific points over a given area, but story maps describe the journey to get from one place to the other. They can be verbal or visual and use landmarks on the path as marker points to guide the way along the route. Pilgrims used to use such maps to travel all the way to the Holy Land, and we all use them when giving directions e.g. Pass the blue house on the left, then turn right at the junction where the old oak tree is etc. etc. Story maps seem more human somehow, more personal.

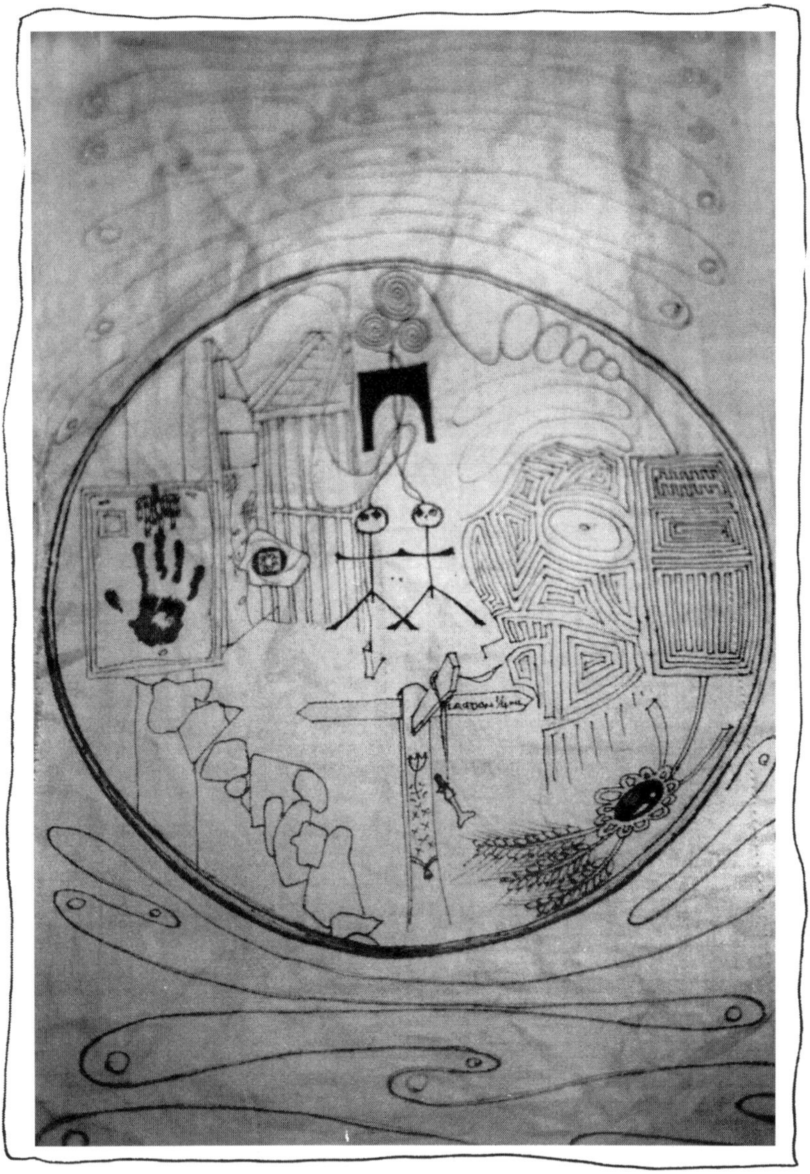

Sigil of Thep-Lan - Sitting in our house by the coast in the West Country, the fire roaring in the stove behind me. The December skies have been threatening rain all day. Even so the wind was whispering in the Monterrey Pines earlier, and I can say I am happy. My wife Francesca is pregnant, first scan next week and the thought takes me back to writing **NTWICCM**. When we wrote that book my first wife Rachel was pregnant with my daughter Eleanor, and much of the magical work was concerned with the birth of a magical child - 'Thep-Lan'. Conjured into the world to bring about the best outcome for all. I couldn't possibly conjure something like that up and hope it to work so I passed over my will to that of the Holy Guardian Angel, and hoped he could do better. The book gave birth to Thep-Lan into the world and I have the sneeking suspicion that all this is Thep-Lan manifesting itself.

Since setting Thep-Lan free (for over 15 years now), magically and spiritually I have been travelling along the plant medicine path. Working with the spirits[1] of Ayahuasca and Peyote, Sao Pedro and

---

1. We could talk of these substances as thought forms, archetypes, plants, entheogens, psychedelics or drugs, but the language that most accurately describes the experience of meeting them is that of magic; where they are viewed as spiritual entities outside of oneself, with their own agenda. Spirits and beings.

Santa Maria as a gateway towards greater association; towards the connecting of myself with what is not my 'self'. Receiving their teachings and their healing. In the UK the taking of any psychedelic substance is illegal unless permitted under license by the Government. However, this is not the case in other countries around the world. My path with these plant medicines has taken me through Brazil where The Church of Santo Daime, and many indigenous tribes, are legally allowed to conduct their ceremonies which include the drinking of ayahuasca; Peru, where the use of ayahuasca is perfectly legal, and enshrined in constitutional rights; to Mexico where I have spent time with the Waxirika people whose way of life is integral to their beliefs concerning peyote and who are legally allowed to conduct peyote ceremonies.

Once I had opened myself to the plant medicine spirits, I would describe their influence as integral, interconnected and inseparable from myself, and their influence on the activities outlined in this book, whether their physical presence was present in our bodies or not, is immaterial. We are associated at the hip! So it is difficult to determine the extent of these plant spirits' influences on the magical walks we undertook all that time ago, and also my hindsight view of the walks now.

Now, this plant medicine path, it really isn't for everyone. But by talking openly about it I hope to offer my own personal experience as a visual story; and as I can only relate my own personal experience as visual imagery personal to me, it really doesn't mean it will resonate with anyone else at all. It isn't necessarily representative of anyone else's inner world, visions or experience.

I believe my work with plant medicines has given me the opportunity to work with the metaphorical and mythical dimension through the visions these medicines bring. With the help of these plant allies this physical dimension of landscape and place and the mythical dimension can co-exist, come together, join, become one.

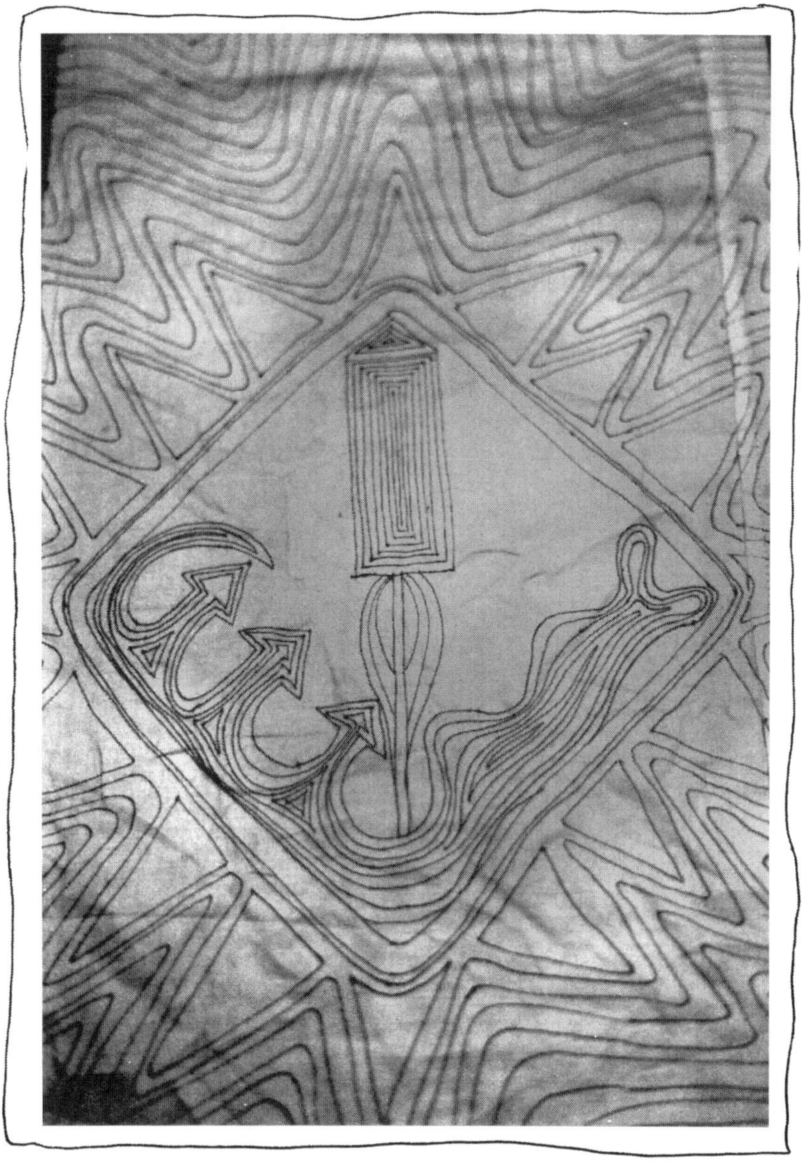

The Black Cat - was the first, no second, spirit I ever encountered in ayahuasca visionary space. I was stood in a room with white walls, the floor covered in sand. A condor (that elusive first spirit!) buried itself in the sand near my feet and over in the far corner of the room stood a cartoon cat, like in a Hannah-Barbera cartoon. "Aaaw. Look over there, a sweet cartoon cat", I pointed. At which point the cat became a black jaguar. It turned, looked at me and promptly opened its mouth WIDE, showing its enormous, sharp teeth and jumped at me; tearing me apart. Pain, fear and vomiting followed, and for the following year every time I drank ayahuasca the black jaguar appeared and ripped me apart. I tried everything to stop it; fight it, run from it, cast spells at it and every time it brushed aside whatever the strategy was and ate me. Again and again.

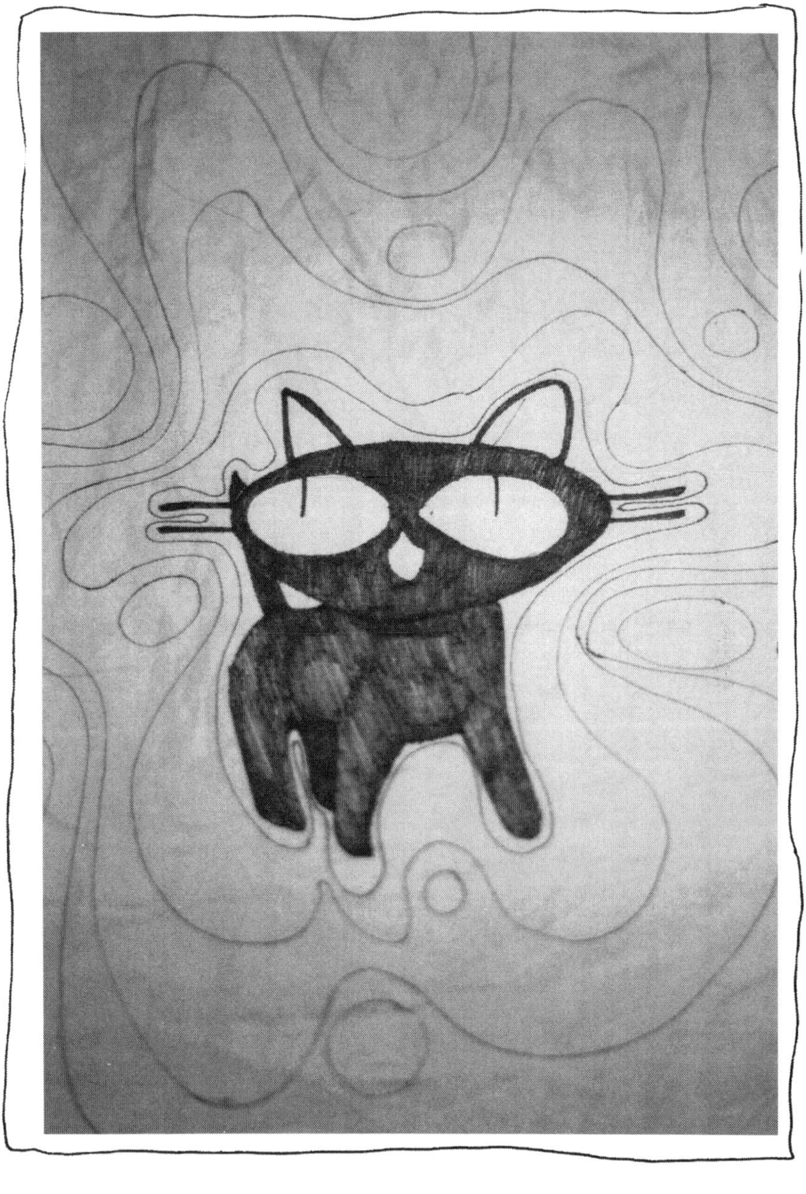

Jaguar - Through the plant medicine visions I believe I was given the opportunity to see the energetic parts of myself as externalised physical beings. This enabled me to interact with tricky, difficult and at times downright terrifying parts of myself in a very real way. If I could interact with these spirits then I could have a relationship with them. When studying demonology for *NTWICCM*, a teacher told me that you should interact with the spirits in a way that you would for other human beings, and if someone is intimidating you in this world, how would you deal with that?

The question for me was, "How can I stop the Jaguar from ripping me apart?", "How do I establish boundaries in a good, loving yet strong way?", and, "If I can't do it on my own who the heck do I trust enough to ask for help?"

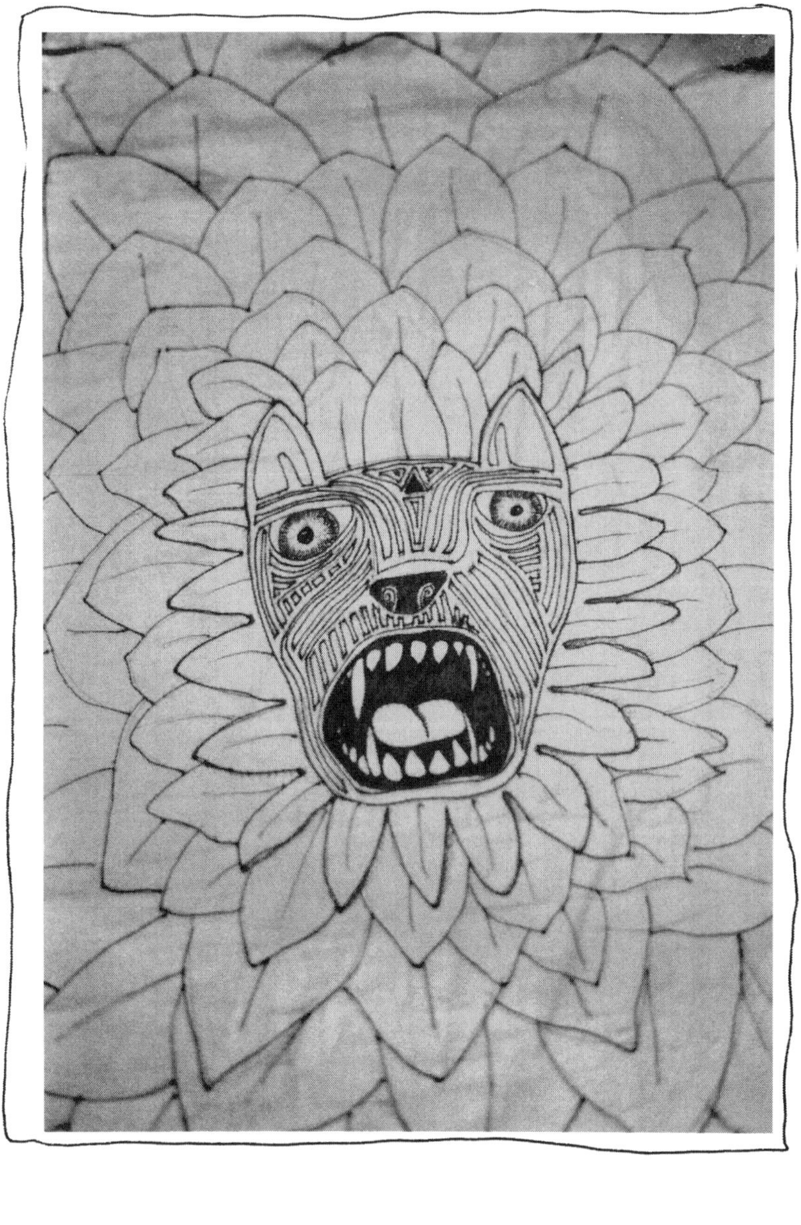

The Lamb - To be strong is a strange concept in our Western culture; we associated it with being 'hard' and the two are not the same in other cultures. The plant medicine way as I have experienced is the way of the hummingbird; and in the mythology of the peyote eating Mayan/Mexica of Mexico the hummingbird is the warrior spirit. It is the only creature living in the forest that is not scared of anything, *and doesn't want anything to be scared of it.* It is fearless; going anywhere with its flashing blue, green and red wings, bringing light, a smile and joy. When the Spanish invaded the area we call Mexico they interpreted this in a way that the hummingbird spirit was the God of War, but I would describe it as a Warrior of Love.

In our Western European culture we tend to think of "strong" and "hard" as synonymous, but they are not. To be strong can also be soft, gentle and loving; firm in your love, firm in your gentleness, regardless of the harshness of the world around you. When the jaguar lies down with the lamb, the cat appears. Calm, inquisitive and silent it is a good guide for me in the inner realms. It is a reminder to me to be super calm, super gentle, super loving and super strong in all my words and actions. The jaguar is the herald reminding me to invoke that gentle warrior spirit. For me it doesn't appear as a hummingbird, but as a lamb carrying the pennant of a red cross on a white background. The jaguar is the call to invoke the lamb.

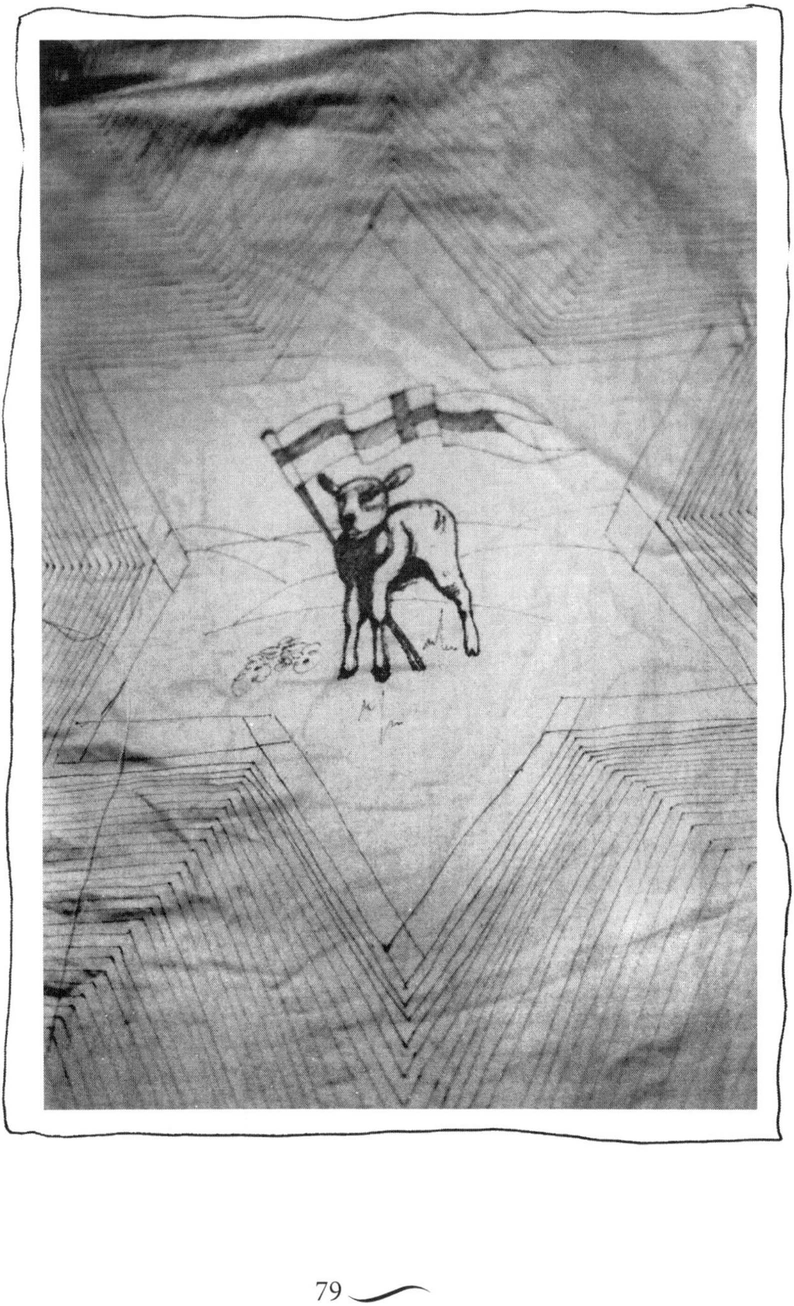

The Passage - I realised that if I could bring some healing, or live in good relationship with these spirits (which were parts of myself after all) then I could bring some kind of healing to the parts of myself that were suffering. For example, my journey of being hunted by the jaguar and the invocation of the lamb in visionary space cleared something I can only describe as an energetic block in my lower back. A painful and at times debilitating injury that had led me to chiropractors, physiotherapists and healers of all sorts for ten years. Since then I can honestly say that I have only been to see anyone about the injury once. In this way the plant medicine brings the opportunity for healing on many levels, but we still have to do the work of the healing itself.

In the Santo Daime Church, this difficult exploration of the inner world is known as, "The Passagem", or Passage. Over the course of drinking ayahuasca in the Santo Daime context for several ceremonies, participants are challenged by their own demons. The challenge of the initiation is to be able to successfully overcome them, and the way in which you overcome them is a personal story to you. For me it felt as if I was being placed on a rack and pulled apart. Drowning in a sea of my own soul wrenching pain, floundering in the turbulent waters. It felt like many days I was there.

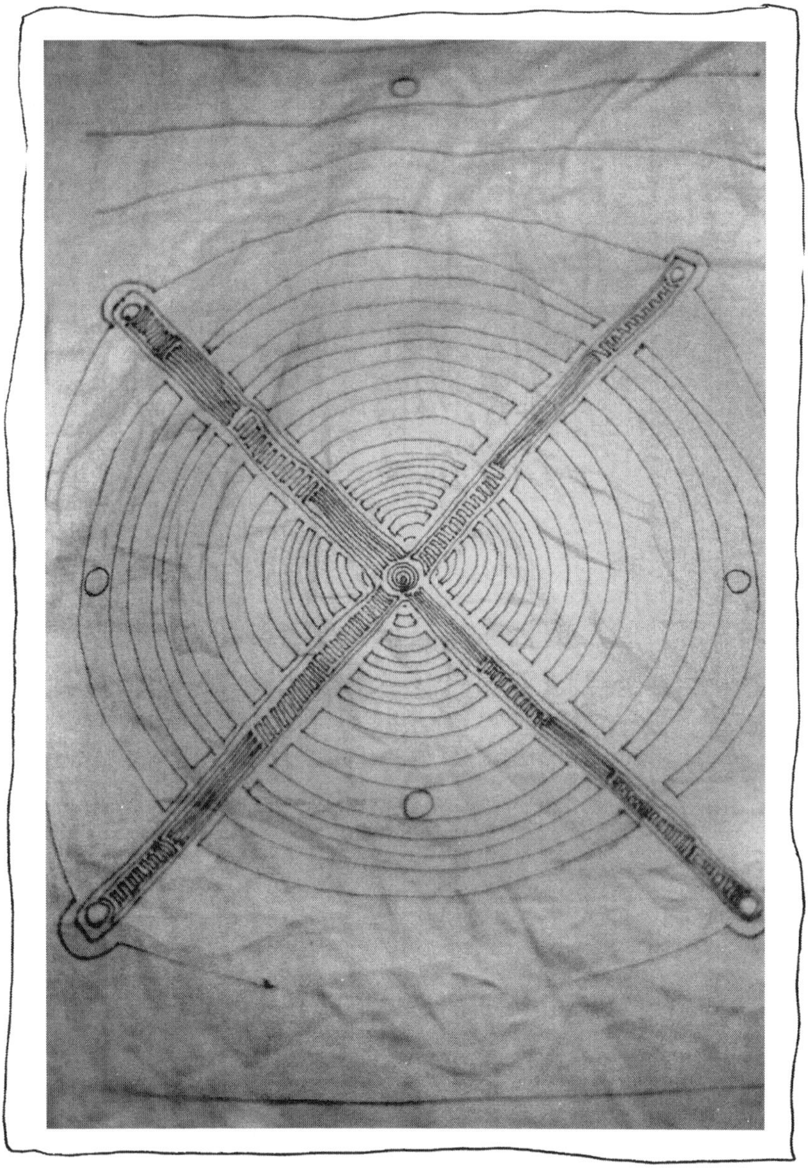

The Great Ship Aceropunta - In between sessions I would research anything I could that could help me in the visions, and it was here I first saw the paintings of Pablo Amaringo. One of his visionary paintings shows the Great Ship Aceropunta. One of the large paddle steamers that travel up and down the Amazon, with pink dolphins in its wake and passengers who were all healers of many different types. Somehow I remembered this as I wallowed in the sea of my own vision. Drowning in fear it came ploughing through the waves towards me, the great ship Aceropunta, white and shining with its Captain and crew dressed in ceremonial white uniforms and caps. They reached down and pulled me out of the water, hauling me onto the deck. There, I saw many healers who were working on people. One came over to me with glowing blue hands. He placed them on my back either side of the spine between the shoulder blades, and I felt his hands going into me. Readjusting the patterns that were running through where my body used to be. Fixing it, and then simply withdrawing. Leaving a print of where the hands had been on my back. I have not been to a physio, or chiropractor complaining of a frozen shoulder since.

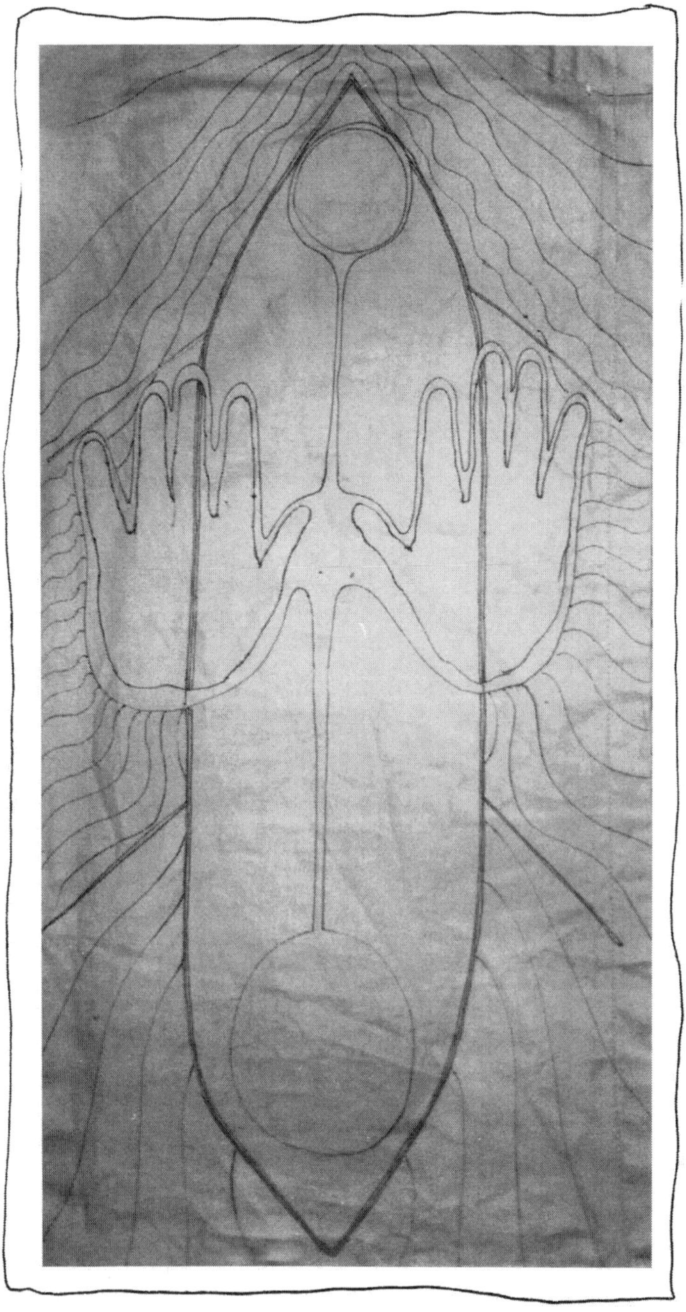

The Star - In The Church of Santo Daime I received my star, became a *fardado*. I chose to take this star for myself once I could dance in the ceremonies, sing the songs in Portuguese and play maraca. It is voluntarily taken when a commitment is made to follow the path of Mestre Irenieu (1892 - 1971).

Over 7ft tall, Mestre Raimundo Irineu Serra was the son of emancipated African-Brazilian slaves. Born in Maranhão in the northeast of Brazil, when he was eighteen years old he migrated 5,000km westward to work in the rubber plantations of the Amazon rainforest, finally arriving in Rio Branco, a town at the junction of Brazil, Bolivia and Peru.

Brazil

Ceu Da Mapia

Rio Branco

Bolivia   **Peru**

Here he found work in several jobs trying to earn a living until he got very, very ill... he tried everything to get better, without success, until he heard that a local indigenous tribe had some medicine that could help him, so he sought them out. The medicine he found was ayahuasca and their cure for him was to undertake a 40-day solo retreat in the jungle with only the ayahuasca to guide him. Here he received a series of visions from a spiritual being that he called The Queen of the Forest, or The Lady of The Conception[1]. She gave to him spiritual teachings in which the drinking of the sacramental ayahuasca was central to the worship of God. She told him to take the ayahuasca out of the jungle and into the towns where it was needed.

He returned to Rio Branco with the ayahuasca and from the 1930s started to hold healing sessions in his house, working with people who came to him for healing. So began the Santo Daime Church and a whole area of Rio Branco is now named Irineu Serra in his honour.

---

1. When the slaves came to Brazil from Africa they were not allowed to worship the nature beings (Orishas) from their own lands. They were forced into Catholicism, but pragmatically they said "OK, well this being we call Yemanja (Goddess of the waves and holotropic ocean) is sort of like the Virgin Mary. So we will say that Yemanja hides behind the mask of the Virgin Mary, and call her the Virgin Mary. What is important is to feel the energy behind the mask and connect with that. Once that is done what the spirit is called does not matter."

The Seal of Solomon - Outwardly the star is a golden, six-pointed metal badge pinned over the heart during ceremonies. In its centre is the image of a condor flying over a crescent moon. Inwardly, to me at least, it represented the energy from above merging with the energy below. Daath in Yesod bringing the knowledge of spirituality into the imaginative realms. Two interpenetrating triangles, representing the merging of Heaven and the Earth. It is also this world and the Otherworld joining, and in these walks the Otherworld and our Middle Earth becoming one for a time.

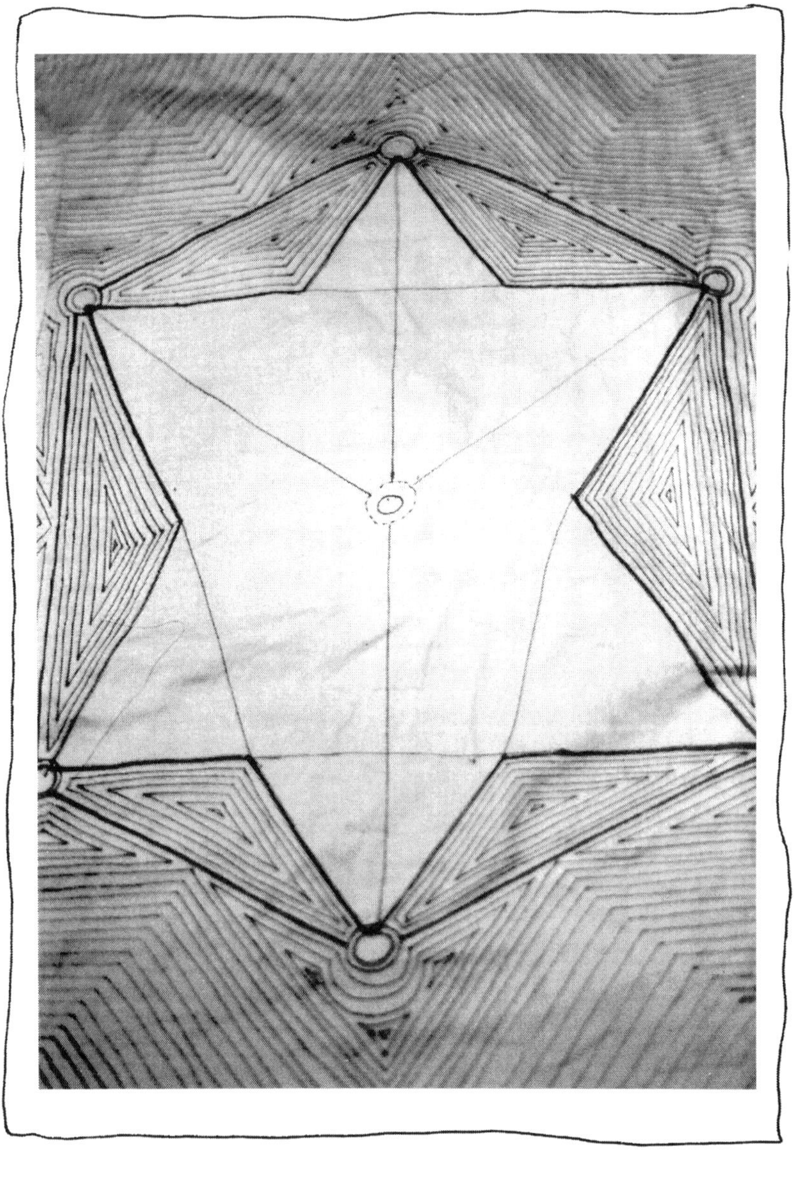

Tiphareth - Albion awakening at the heart of the Kabbalah, centre of all things, all Worlds. The central world of the Sephiroth is the place of love, of association and coming together. It is called Tiphareth.

With ayahuasca as my guide, the prayer flags tell the story of my journey to get there, to that Holy Place in this green and pleasant land.

This is the song I wanted to sing to the Dead. Letting the wind over Roughtor carry the ballad of my life to William Newbound and my other ancestors.

And now, my song is sung.

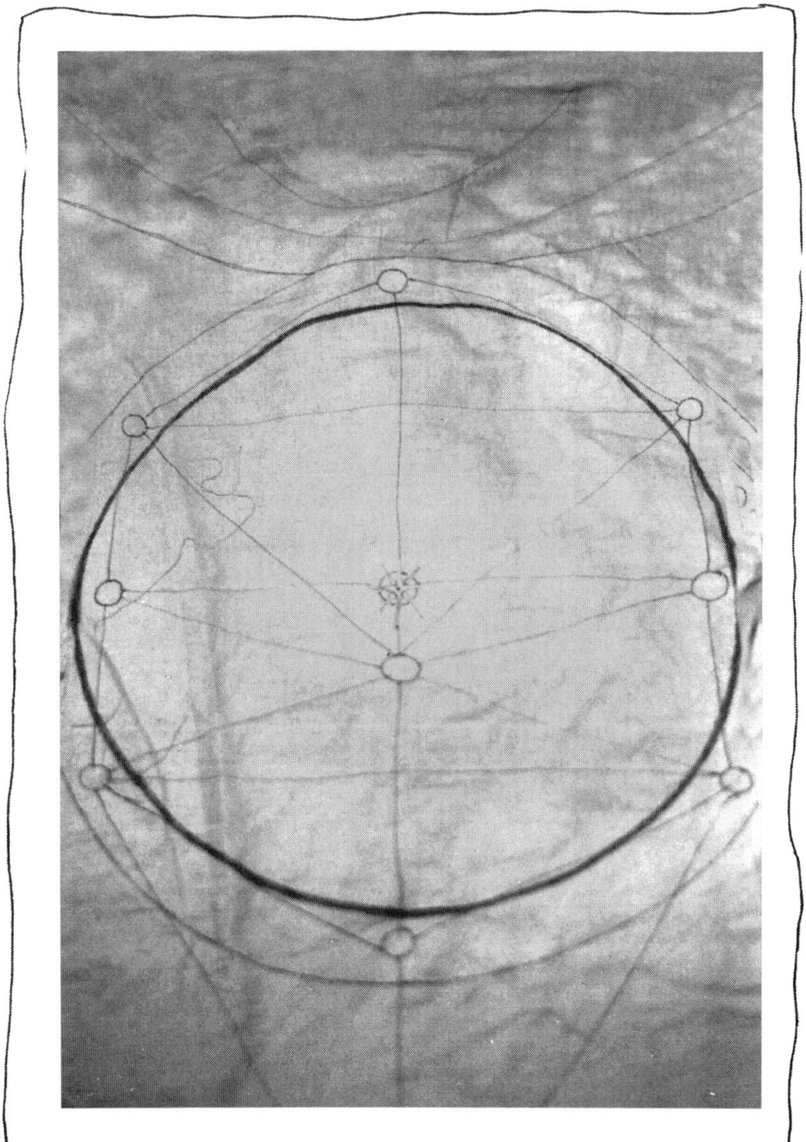

PART III
Photographs

HARTLAND POINT

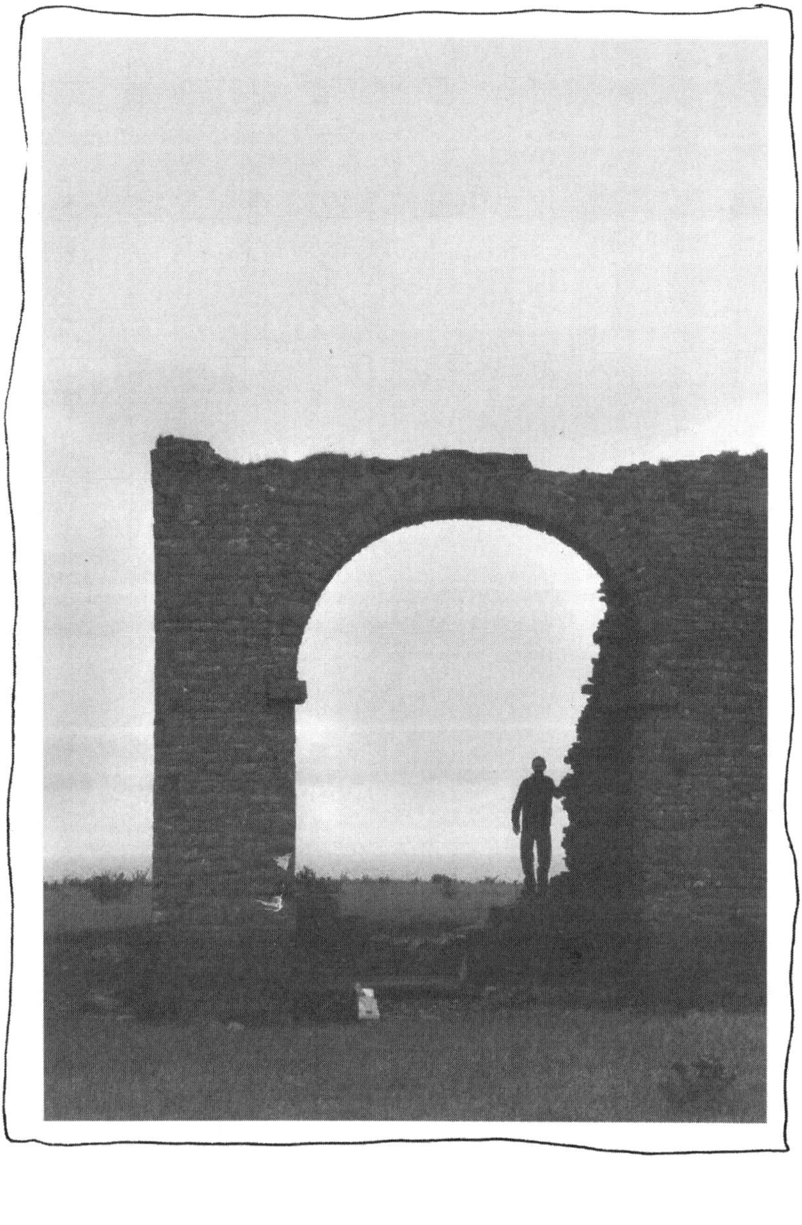

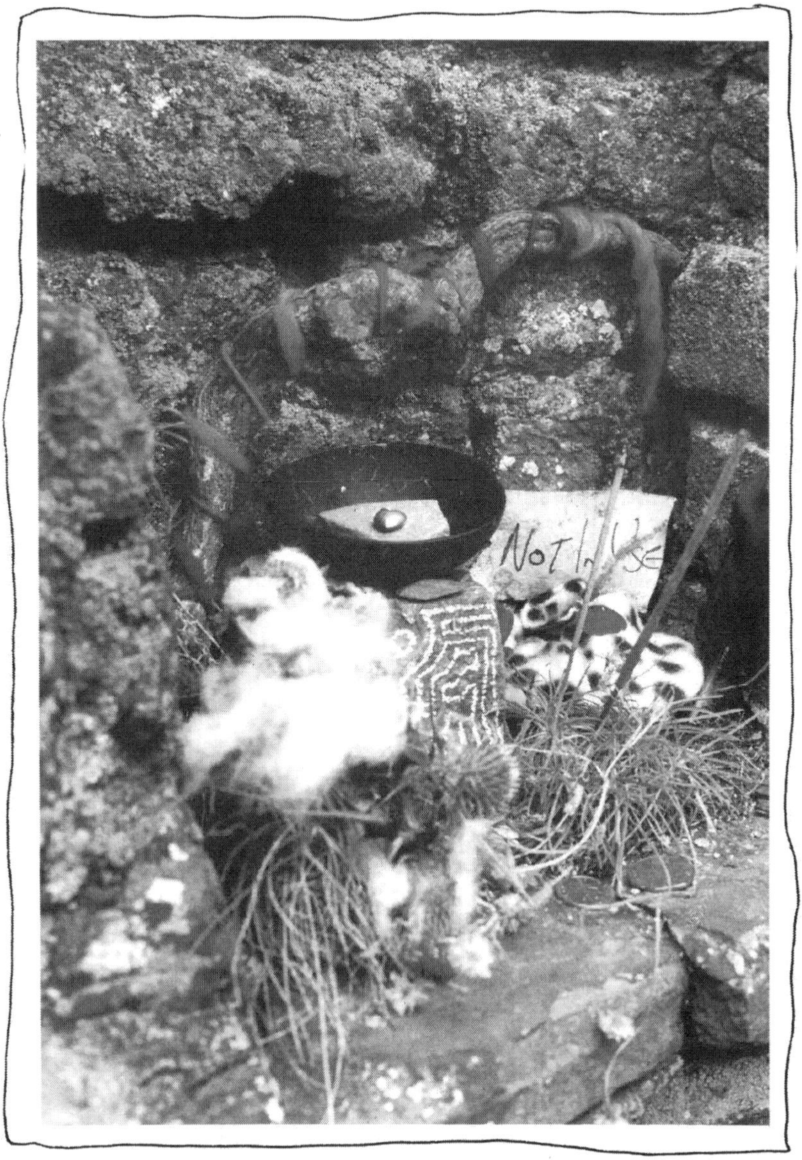

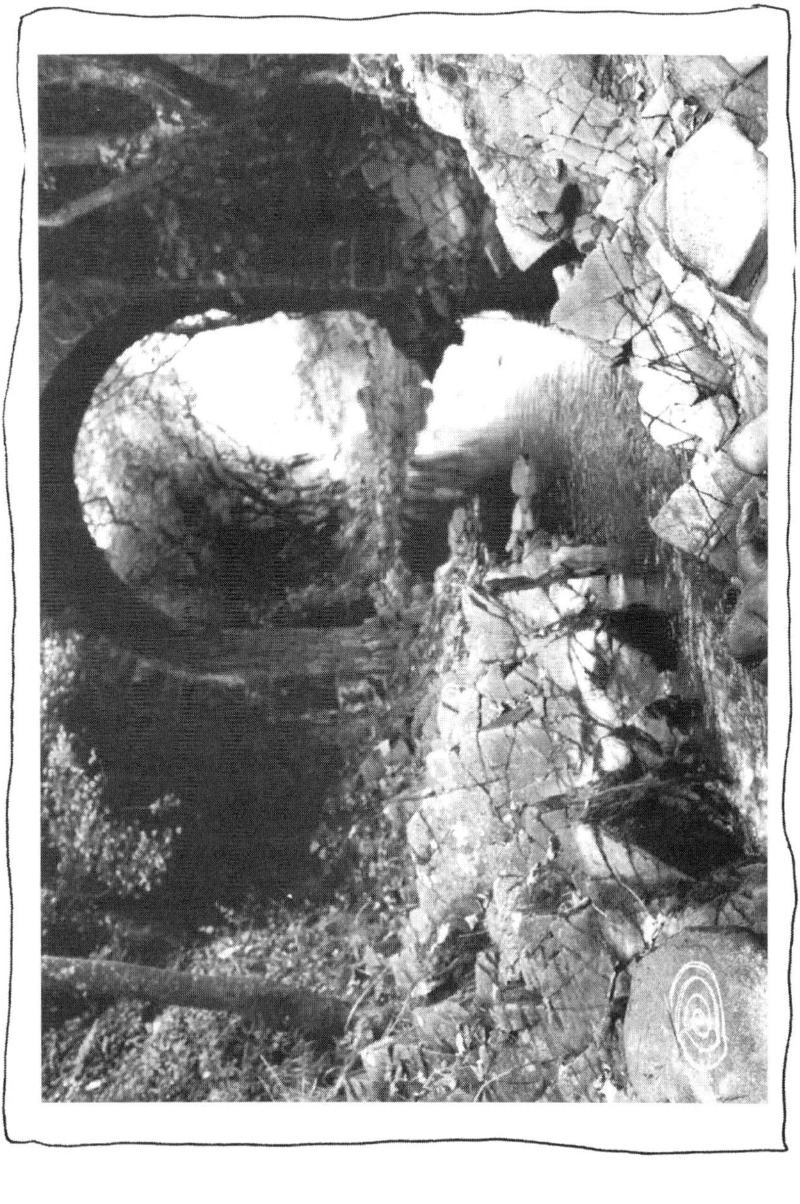

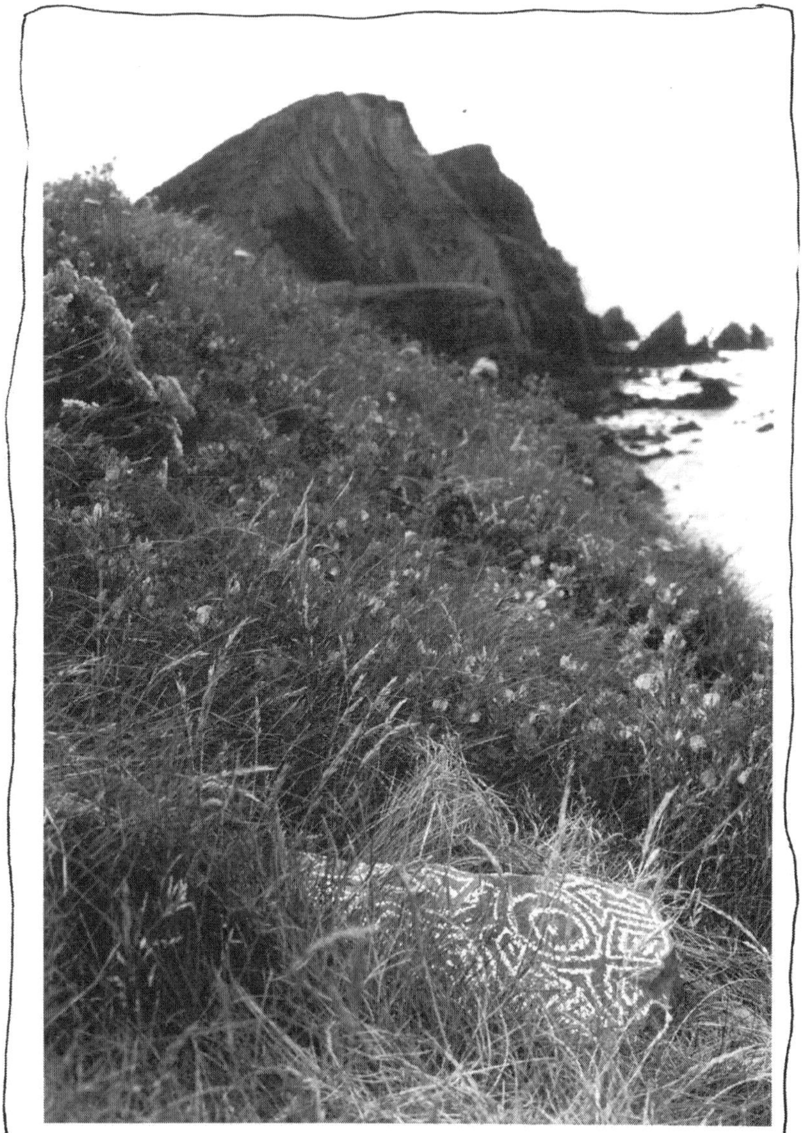

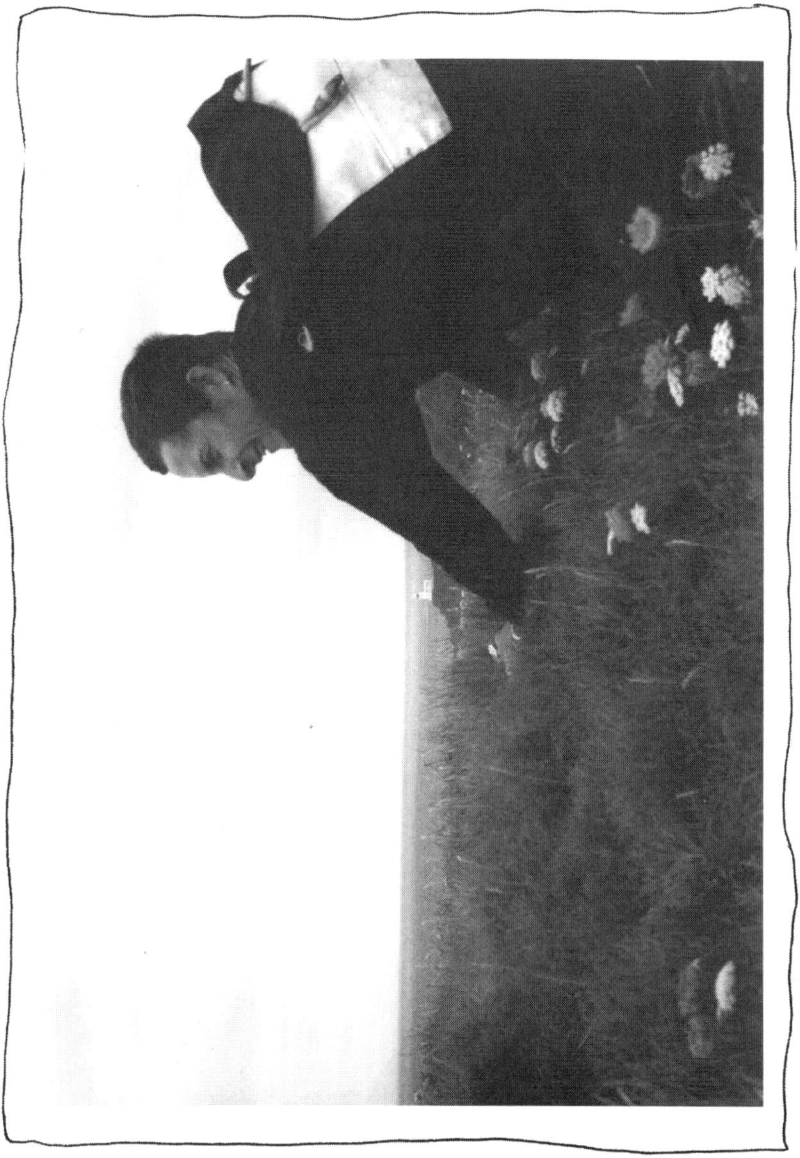

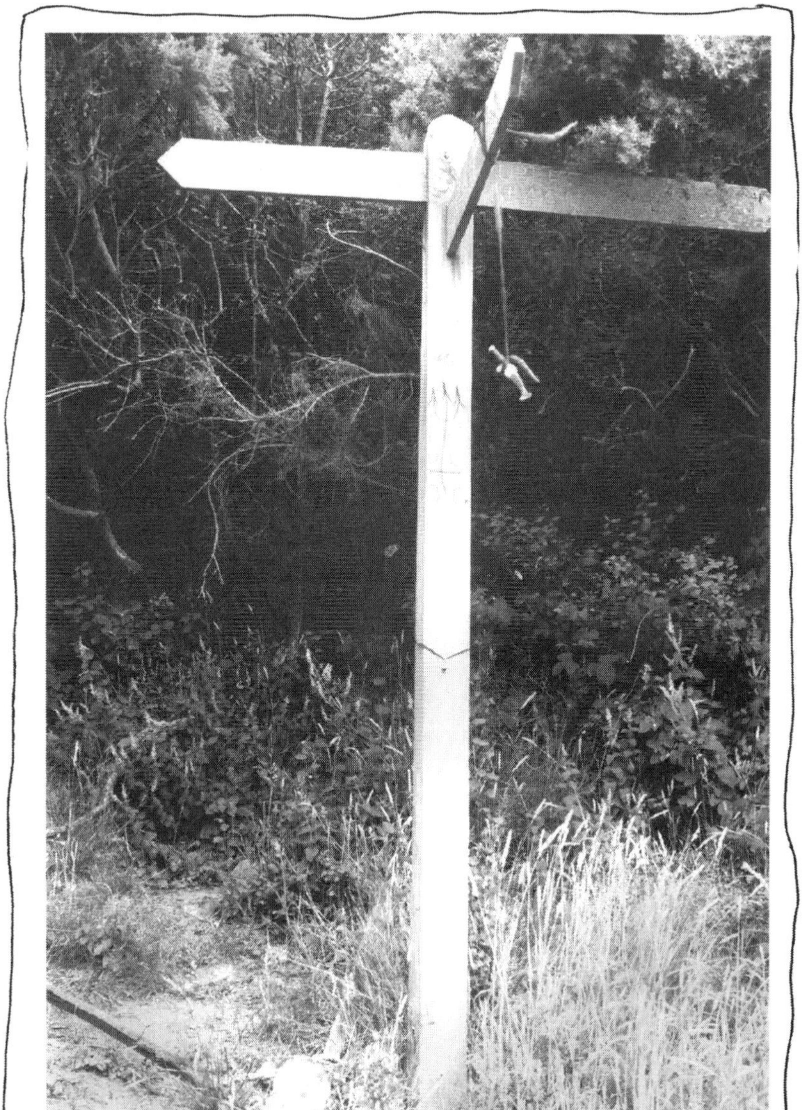

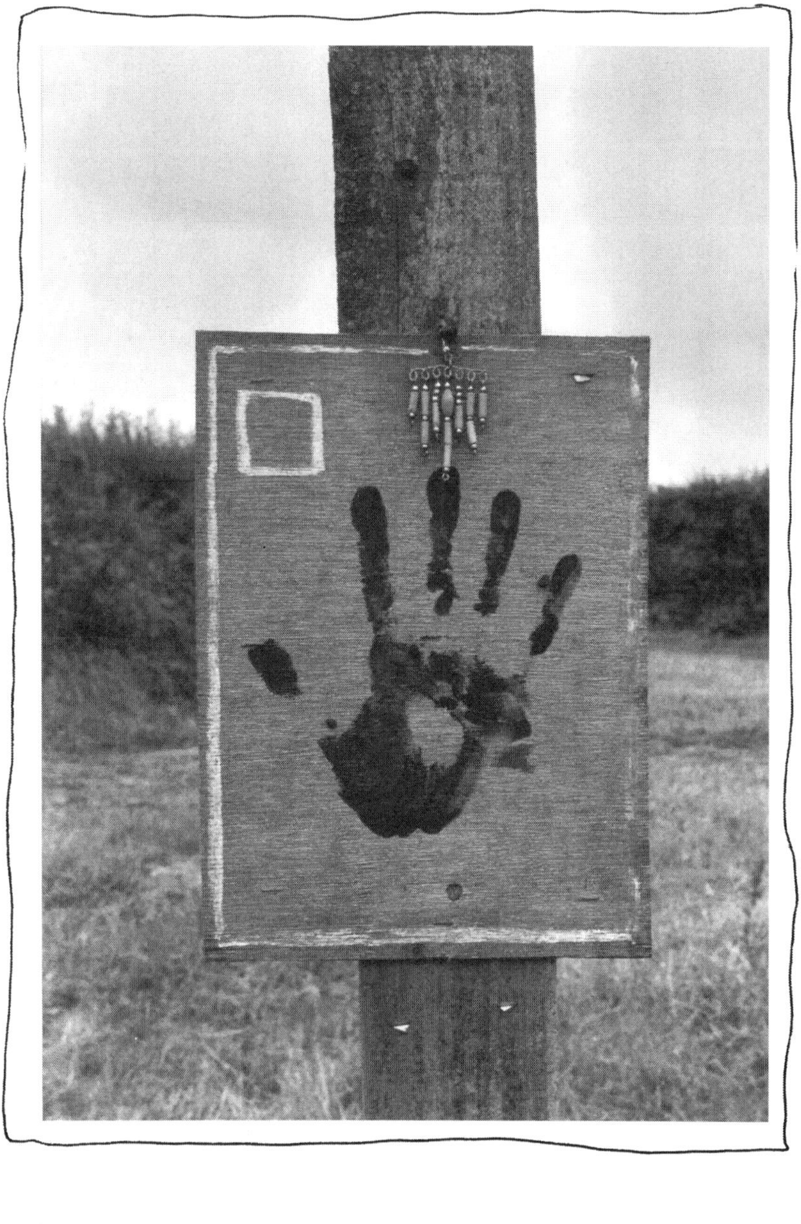

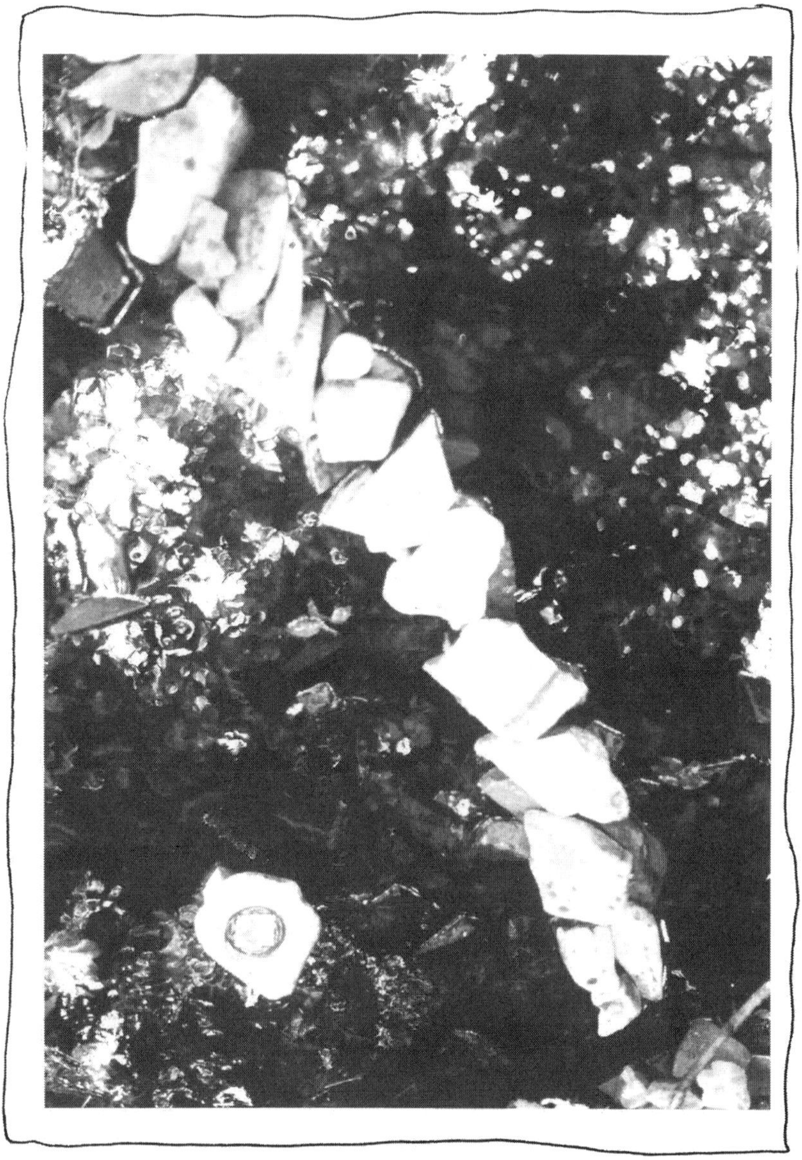

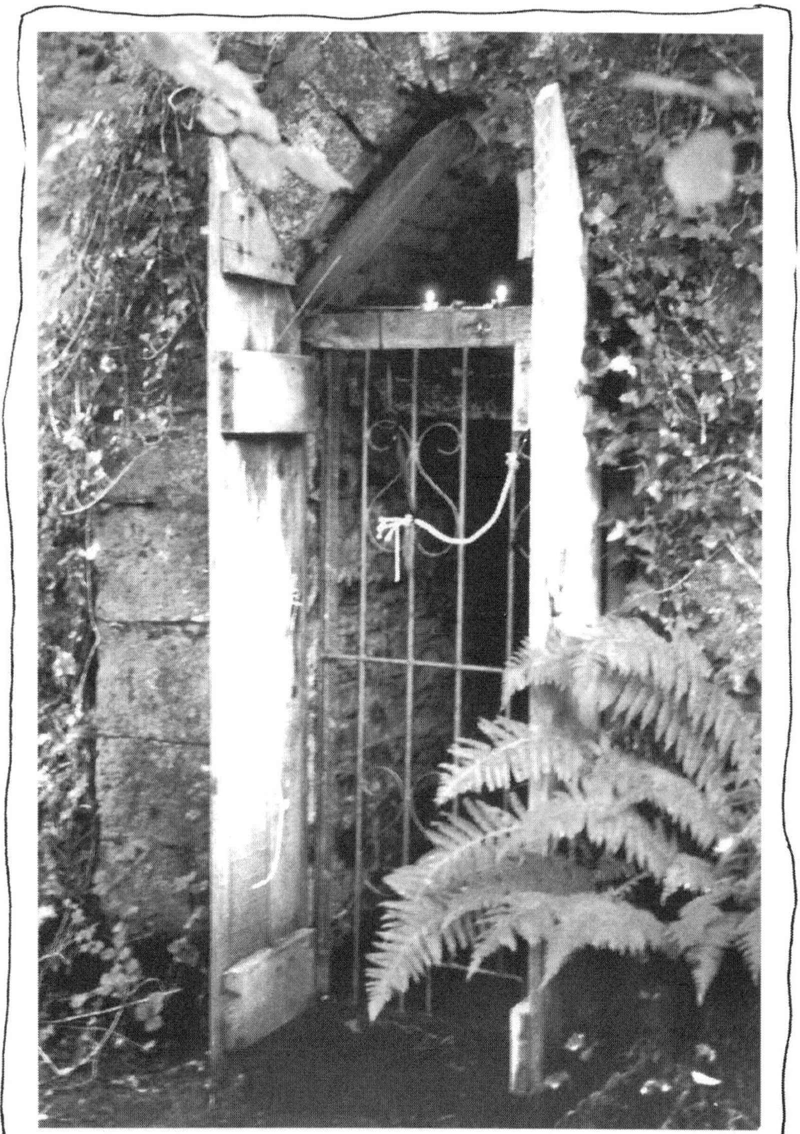

ROUGHTOR

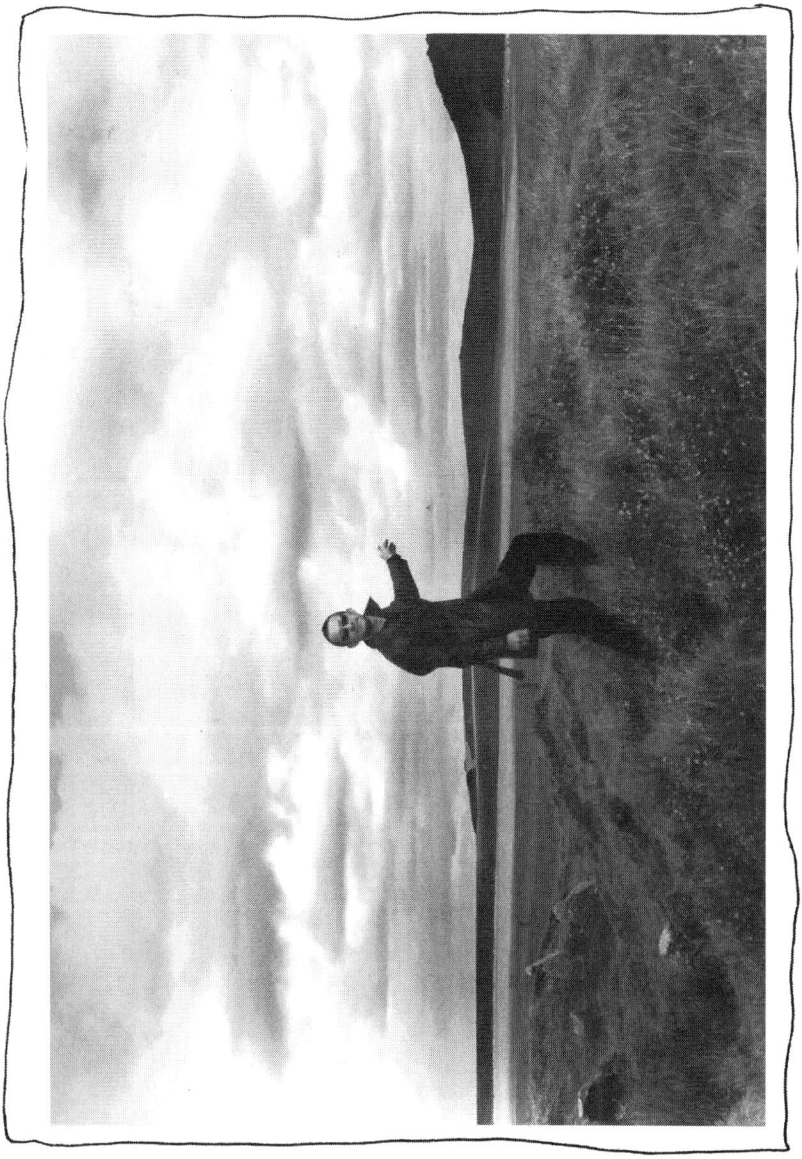

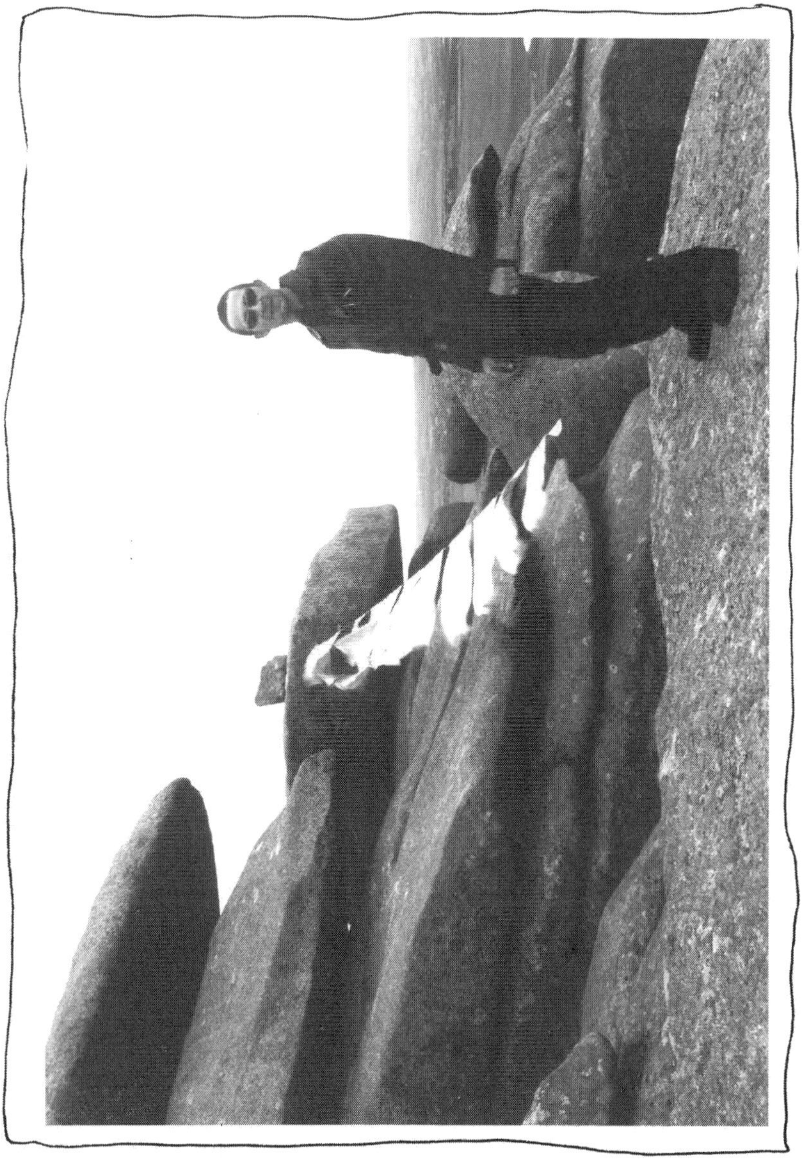

Julian Vayne is an occultist and author of numerous texts in the academic and underground press. In his professional work Julian develops approaches to encourage curiosity in settings such as historic buildings, museums, galleries and landscapes. His fascination with altered states has led him to explore techniques of changing consciousness ranging from the highly formalized ritual drama of Freemasonry through to the trance methods of witchcraft and the emerging freestyle shamanism of the modern psychedelic age. Julian is a leading contributor to theblogofbaphomet.com

Greg Humphries is an artist living in West Cornwall who spends his time connecting people to Nature and The Spirit of Place through art, outdoor education and woodland management via his company Future Tracks (www.futuretracks.co.uk). His interest in the nature-based belief systems of indigenous communities has led him to be in ceremony with people in the Amazon, the Arctic, Central Mexico and Sherwood Forest. The knowledge he found in these places is used in his practice to re-awaken our relationship with the spirits of these islands.

Printed in Great Britain
by Amazon